DOG TRAINING MADE EASY

DOG TRAINING
MADE EASY
for You and Your Dog

By Wm. Cary Duncan

ILLUSTRATED BY ERNEST H. HART

BELL PUBLISHING COMPANY, INC.
NEW YORK

TO THE MEMORY OF
RICHARD BUSH ADAMS
WHO TAUGHT ME THAT DOGS DESERVE
BOTH OUR AFFECTION AND OUR RESPECT

This edition published by Bell Publishing Company, Inc.,
a division of Crown Publishers, Inc.,
by arrangement with Little, Brown and Company

Q   R   S

Contents

DOG TRAINING MADE EASY

CHAPTER I

By Way of Introduction

I'M told that to be a good talker you must have something worth while to say and adapt your way of saying it to the particular person or persons you're talking to. This formula sounds so simple I'm going to try it.

What I have to say is worth while, I think, because if I can say it intelligently enough, it should help create a better understanding between you and your dog or between you and dogs in general. This, in turn, should be worth while because people and dogs are so much alike in many ways and have so many interests in common that they ought to know each other — not casually only, nor as master and slave, but intimately and on something like equal terms, as good friends and companions.

As for the particular people I'm talking to, or would be if I could, I know exactly who they are. They are the men, women and children who own a dog or dogs, hope to own one sometime, or have given up all hope of ever owning one, yet love dogs just the same. And I especially wish the readers of this book might include the occasional persons who have no interest whatever in dogs, or even positively dislike or fear them. Because, as already implied, they are missing something we all prize: the possession of a true friend. And it's just possible these pages might make them appreciate that fact.

Those in the last group are becoming fewer all the time. This is especially true here in the Americas, where more and more of us each year realize our inalienable right to life, liberty and the pursuit of a runaway pup, and are making the most of it. As a result we have reached a point where to us, as to our ancestors in the British Isles and on the Continent, a dog is no longer just a dog, but is spotted on sight as a mere mongrel or as a purebred representative of an officially recognized breed. If the former, he attracts little or no notice. If the latter, he usually receives the recognition and attention he deserves. For we have learned by experience that the commonly understood but unscientific phrase, "Blood will tell," is the truth; and that, when blood cannot be traced back for generations, it may tell a very sad story to people who buy pups they fondly believe will develop into dogs to be proud of.

Dogs, as animals go, are not long-lived. Individuals have been known to approach thirty, a few reach twenty or over, but ten is the average for dogs that reach maturity at all. When your old pal finally passes on, you usually look for a successor as nearly like him as possible. Your chances of finding what you're looking for are much greater if the favorite was a registered dog and the new pup not only belongs to the same breed but, if you are willing to take a little trouble, may even be a near relative. Such a pup has something behind him besides his tail — he has a background of carefully recorded ancestors whose characteristics he is pretty sure to inherit. Which is why, to perpetrate an Irish bull, background should be very much in the foreground when you make your choice.

This growing interest in dogs of distinction is no respecter of persons. The unimpressive old gentleman sitting next you in the subway or the suburban bus may be a fancier with a national reputation. So may the leader of your favorite orchestra, the farmer who brings your fresh eggs, the pastor of your church or the president of your local bank. In the big parade of those who know a good dog when they see one, the man who reads the *Wall Street Journal* and the man who reads your gas meter are on precisely the same plane.

As for the women, when they scrapped sugar-coated novels and the sewing circle, shed long skirts and slipped more or less gracefully into slacks, they brought to the dog game the same enthusiasm that has been a lifesaver for various other sporting activities formerly reserved for men. For ladies love dogs as naturally as a film favorite loves her fan mail — and their love is no longer blind. Today they are among our staunchest sticklers for correct breed type and know a canine king from a commoner as well as, and often better than, their menfolk.

For this, field trials and bench shows are largely responsible. The latter, although originally confined to the exhibition of gun dogs and hounds, were made to order to attract the modern woman. So it's not surprising that the sporting breeds now supply less than 50 per cent of the entries or that feminine fanciers are making a strong bid for leadership in both personal and financial support of the shows.

Meanwhile Young America, as usual, has not allowed itself to be forgotten. It has its children's classes, to which only purebreds are eligible and in which the youngsters pose their pets under the critical eyes of experts who award special ribbons and prizes for clever handling.

Obedience tests, the latest innovation, have already become popular. Like the children's classes they are open to purebreds of all varieties and call for a specified series of tests, with wins counting as points toward the official titles, Companion Dog, Companion Dog Excellent and Utility Dog.

These events have been an eye opener. If you have a notion, for instance, that very little dogs lack brains, you will be interested to learn that in at least one of these events, a tiny Chihuahua, weighing a scant two pounds, came, saw and conquered a ringful of competitors, several of which were more than thirty-five times his size.

But although officially licensed bench shows draw a yearly entry of over 80,000 (of which a certain percentage are repeats), they are only a small corner of the picture. Registrations in our two leading studbooks alone number more than 100,000 every twelve months; and statistics show that they represent less than one in ten eligible dogs. So if we estimate the average life of these bluestockings conservatively at three years, we must figure their number in North America at any given time as at least 3,000,000.

And that's only a starter. Nondescripts still have the call, to the tune of better than five to one — probably ten to one would be more nearly correct. In New York City alone, a place peculiarly unsuited to the extensive ownership of dogs, the canine population tops 300,000; and a rock-bottom estimate for the whole country gives us the almost unbelievable total of 18,000,000 dogs of all races, colors and conditions of servitude.

That sort of popularity is never achieved by mere chance. Yet most dogs do no real work, as horses used to do, and apparently serve no useful purpose, like cattle, sheep and hogs. How account for the high position a dog holds? Evidently he has something very definite and unusual to sell, and I think I know what it is. To the best of my knowledge and belief he is the only animal that instinctively prefers the society of human beings to that of his own kind; and, if the Bible is to be trusted, we all love those who love us.

This inborn affinity for man was originally, in all probability, a latent characteristic, but so strong that it required only a few generations of domestication to bring it out. For the earliest carvings show that prehistoric dogs possessed it. Nowadays it is highly developed, as anyone who has ever raised a litter of puppies will testify. Tiny toddlers, less than ten days old, and before their eyes are open, not only have no fear of human beings; they will leave their mother and the nice warm dinner she is providing to go to them.

Contrast this with the behavior of a newborn calf, left hidden in a brushy pasture by its dam. At your approach it instantly takes advantage of the protective undergrowth in which it lies, crouching close to the ground, remaining absolutely motionless and watching you with big, frightened eyes. When it realizes you have discovered its hiding place it leaps to its feet in terror and dashes away through the birches and alders exactly as a wild fawn will do, showing surprising speed for such a baby. Thousands of years of domesticated ancestry have not overcome its instinctive fear of man.

This congenital distrust of humans is evident in nearly all our farm animals, even after they are fully grown. The gentlest and cleverest of mares with a newborn foal at her side will bear watching. In many cases even her favorite groom must keep his eyes open or keep his distance. Occasionally female dogs are equally apprehensive about the safety of their pups, but only occasionally, and practically never when their owners or people they know are involved.

Dogs have another characteristic unusual enough to be mentioned. Their intelligence almost never makes them untrustworthy. Among animals, this is an exception that helps to prove a rule. A rogue elephant is doubly dangerous because his native cunning enables him to plan his crimes with well-nigh incredible craft. A mule is more treacherous than a horse because he knows more. In Spain a fighting bull that survives his first appearance in a ring never plays a return engagement. The knowledge gained in one short set-to makes him too dangerous for even the most expert matador to meet.

It's just the opposite with dogs. The more they know, the more dependable they are. Nine times out of ten it's subnormal mentality that makes biters and snappers. They snap and bite with the silly idea it's necessary for self-defense. They haven't brains enough to realize human beings are their friends.

But the two fundamental reasons I've given only begin to explain man's really remarkable affection for a so-called dumb animal — an affection so nearly universal it has made "Love me, love my dog" a proverb. The answer is to be found in a combination of canine traits whose appeal is almost as elusive and difficult to define as that which binds us to our human friends. Perhaps the simplest way to put it is this: man has a good working knowledge of the mental and emotional equipment of many domestic animals; dogs are the only animals, domestic or otherwise, that seem not only to understand, but actually to sympathize with the thoughts and feelings of man. It will require but a few days', or it may be even hours', association with the first puppy or grown dog you can call your own to convince you of this significant and fascinating fact.

CHAPTER II

Why "Puppy Preferred" Is a Good Buy

SINCE you have opened this book and are reading this paragraph, it is sensible to assume that you belong to one of the four classes mentioned in my introductory chapter.

If you have never owned a dog, but are about to buy one, or if you have been fortunate enough to receive your first puppy as a present, the suggestions contained in this chapter may be welcome. Even if you have been a dog owner for years, you may be interested to check the points at which you and I agree and disagree. For an honest difference of opinion, like honest confession, is good for the soul. But I am beginning this book with the assumption that you are a beginner too, and that we face our respective problems on an equal footing.

Naturally a gift dog, like a gift horse, is not to be looked in the mouth; but if you pay for this latest addition to your family, by all means buy a purebred: if you're wise, you will decide on a pup rather than a grown-up. A pedigree may add a few dollars to the original cost, but from then on it's a stand-off; and we have already learned why an authentic record of ancestry is worth much more than the paper it's printed or written on.

Your choice of a puppy less than four months old will prove a happy one for two reasons. The first is a matter of ordinary expediency. It's comparatively easy to bring up a pup in the way he should go, but something else again to overcome native faults already fixed or correct bad habits already formed. The second reason goes a little deeper. For even if you were fortunate enough to find a fully grown canine prodigy with neither failings nor flaws, you would miss two of the most interesting and instructive factors in dog ownership — the study of the mental and physical reactions of a growing pup and the liberal education you are bound to acquire from the moment you begin to train him.

Puppies are fascinating subjects for psychoanalysis and their schooling is no one-way street. By making the most of your opportunities you will learn as much as your pupil. If you happen to be a take-everything-for-granted sort of person or a boy or girl in your early teens, you may even learn considerably more than he does; and what you learn may prove fully as useful to you as the puppy's lessons can ever be to him. Let me explain, beginning with the boys or girls in their teens.

One of the qualities we should acquire as early in life as possible is a sense of responsibility. Conscientious parents devise all kinds of schemes to cultivate this trait in their children. Yet few of these devices are more successful than the gift of a pup with the distinct understanding that its welfare and education are to be delegated exclusively to its young master or mistress. For unlike most tasks with the same objective, the feeding, brushing, washing, exercising and training required are not the same old routine chores, to be evaded if possible, but a constant source of interesting amusement. Caring for animals of any kind, old or young, tends to make youngsters (and oldsters, too) less self-centered and selfish.

To cite an extreme example, the superintendent of a home for subnormal and abnormal children told me of a patient — an "introvert" who stubbornly refused to study or play with the other children or so much as notice or speak to them. Even when looking at her picture books this strange child insisted on sitting in a corner, her face to the wall. All the rules of psychiatry were called into play with no effect. But the accidental meeting of this little girl and a cocker puppy belonging to one of the resident nurses turned the trick that had a whole staff of experts on mental diseases stumped. By means of the child's almost fanatical affection for the spaniel as a means toward an end she was brought back to normal in less than a month. This by the simple and obvious method of allowing her to play with the only living thing beside herself she could care for, but only on condition the other children joined in the fun.

In the diametrically opposite cases of children who are perfectly normal in other respects but have an inborn and distressing fear of dogs or other animals, the problem is easily solved and a two-months-old pup is the answer. For it is next to impossible for even the most timid child to be more than momentarily afraid of a frolicsome little ball of fur; and the longer the pair associate with each other the more congenial they become. Months before the pup is fully grown his human playmate will almost certainly have lost not only fear of this particular dog but also of dogs in general. Familiarity between a growing child and a growing pup breeds mutual confidence and affection, not contempt.

When it comes to adults, I'm tempted to say that the normal man or woman that doesn't like dogs doesn't know dogs. That may be putting it a trifle strong; so it's probably safer to say that people who have had any considerable association with dogs and still retain any feeling of fear or aversion are exceedingly rare. In this connection some scientists claim that the sensation of fear creates a faint effluvium, much too delicate for human nostrils to detect but which the supersensitive canine nose instantly recognizes and resents. If and when this is true, human and dog are involved in a vicious circle extremely difficult to break.

Both observation and personal experience lead me to believe the theory may have some foundation in fact; for I'm going to confess that when I was a very small boy, my feeling about dogs was a paradox. They frightened me but fascinated me too. Needless to say, my very first puppy put an end to all my misgivings, and I've never been afraid of a normal or moderately abnormal dog since. Among the hundreds I've judged in the show ring, a job that requires a very thorough going-over with the hands from teeth to tail, I've naturally encountered a few pretty tough customers, but have never suffered so much as a scratch deep enough to break the skin. Even the most disagreeable of dogs knows when you're his friend and appreciates the compliment.

All this, while educational, deals with human and dog psychology, an elusive and decidedly mystifying subject that may not interest you a particle. Here's something more tangible. Few of us who live in the city or suburbs get enough exercise; or if we do, it's not the right kind. Pavements are like stern stepfathers compared with the restful and invigorating effect we get from Mother Earth. So we're inclined to ride too much and walk too little, and our waistlines, our livers, and as likely as not our physicians, are constantly reminding us of the fact. Yet most of us are too busy or too indifferent or too something else to do anything about it. If you are in that class a good healthy dog — or better yet, a puppy — will prove a godsend. He needs exercise and plenty of it or he won't be healthy for long, and you'll probably see that he gets it. This means daily walks in the fields or through the park. If you don't happen to care for walking, remember that the less you like it, the more you need it; and the more of it you do, the less you'll dislike it. It's a good gamble that in a week or two you'll begin to get the habit and before you know it will enjoy your outings with Jock as much as he does.

That's a physical angle. Now let's get back to an educational slant that is almost equally practical. While you and I can't be Lord Bacons and take all knowledge for our province, we still like to be fairly well informed about subjects intelligent people are interested in and talk about. Among these is what we call natural history. And this happens to be one field in which, to mix metaphors, the average city or suburban dweller is pretty much at sea. When a college-bred businessman whose operations affect two continents and whose income-tax return looks like a tabloid synopsis of our national debt asks you how many eggs a good hen lays a day, something ought to be done about it; and his dog can help do it.

Of all domestic animals dogs are the most continuously and actively inquisitive. Their wonderfully sensitive noses investigate everything that gives off an intriguing scent, however slight; and anything that moves, if only a falling leaf, interests them. They discover innumerable things you or I would never see. A hike through the countryside or even a stroll in a city park, with a wide-awake puppy or grown dog for company, reminds one of the old-time definition of a liberal education: Mark Hopkins on one end of a log and a boy on the other.

If you're fortunate enough to live in the country the courses offered by the Canine College for Nature Study are almost limitless in scope. If your pup doesn't rout out a rabbit, a weasel or an ovenbird, it will be a mud turtle, a lizard or a wood mouse. Or he strikes the track of a fox and shows you where Reynard put in a busy half hour hunting for field mice or ate a ruffed grouse for dinner. Or you follow him along a brook and learn that mink fish for fun as well as food — that these ruthless mass murderers recognize no closed season and respect no law, destroying every day in the year four times as many fish as they can possibly eat, for the pure pleasure of the kill.

You'll discover the woodchuck has at least two

doors to his den and that, when it comes to caution, he's the original Mr. Milquetoast — so timid he rarely ventures more than a hundred yards from his front porch; yet puts up a whale of a battle when caught unawares and forced to fight his way home.

A hundred such interesting and instructive bits of outdoor lore you will pick up during your daily rambles. It will always be something new, and, to my way of thinking, worth knowing. What's more, you will one day discover you are becoming acquainted with a great many things besides birds and beasts. Unconsciously you have been cultivating a gift for observation that makes you realize there are numberless interesting insects, plants and trees you have seen hundreds of times, but have never taken the trouble to identify or even notice. It is no coincidence that, of all the people I have ever met, the man who knows most about nature and the man who knows most about dogs are one and the same.

CHAPTER III

The Breed to Choose

ASSUMING you are still within easy reading distance, I'm taking it for granted that, other things being equal, you have decided on a puppy instead of a grown dog. Also that you agree mongrels have two obvious assets — and only two. You can get one for little or nothing; and you can have the dubious privilege of guessing what it's going to look like when it grows up. But it's only fair to remind you once more that the fun is all over and the riddle solved in ten months or less, and that the solution is almost always a eugenic slap in the face.

Volunteering advice about your choice of a breed is another matter, and a delicate one. Comparisons between the different varieties of pure-bred dogs have become one of the shortest cuts to social suicide.

To put off the evil paragraphs as long as I conscientiously can, I'm going to suggest that we first take a look at the American Kennel Club's official division of over a hundred breeds into six distinct groups, each group named to indicate in a general way the character of the dogs it includes. So please turn to page 21. You will see that there are enough breeds to satisfy practically anyone's taste, purpose and purse. Yet some varieties are hard to classify.

Take Dalmatians (coach dogs to you and me), which might sensibly be listed in both the sporting and the working groups, as well as in the non-sporting section, where we find them. When we look into their past we discover they were once war dogs, doing duty as sentinels on the borders of Dalmatia and Croatia, and have also been efficient draft dogs and shepherds; while we all know their original specialty was clearing the " 'ard 'ighway" of jaywalkers that otherwise might be run down by hit-and-run drivers of the Tallyho stagecoaches of days gone by. They also have a right to join the sporting group, for they were frequently used as gun dogs and are said to have been better than fair hunters and retrievers.

English bulldogs, also classed as non-sporting, were very definitely sporting when bull baiting was considered a legitimate and perfectly respectable pastime.

As for the terriers, almost every one of the twenty varieties that make up their group was originally a sporting breed. Their very name, taken from the French *terre,* means "earth dogs," or dogs that were used to go to earth — into fox

FUNDAMENTAL CLASSES OF DOGS

1. SPORTING CLASS 2. HOUND CLASS 3. WORKING CLASS
(*English Setter*) (*Beagle*) (*Great Dane*)

4. TERRIER CLASS 5. TOY CLASS 6. NON-SPORTING CLASS
(*Wire-haired Fox Terrier*) (*Pekinese*) (*Bulldog*)

and badger burrows and such — to drive out game that had been run in by hounds. Even today practically all terriers will hunt furred game and hunt it pretty well.

The average cocker spaniel, on the other hand, which took its name from its common use years ago as a woodcock dog in heavy cover, is very rarely used as a gun dog today, although he is once more beginning to come into his own in the field.

Reversing the picture, several of the present Working Group, like Old English sheep dogs, mastiffs, Saint Bernards and Samoyedes (the stunning snow-white fellows most people call "spitz"), turned in their union cards years ago and haven't done a day's work since — not in this country anyway.

As this conflict between classification and actual performance or character is by no means confined to the few examples we have given, it's best not to take this group business too seriously. With few exceptions members of every breed in all six groups may make ideal house dogs. When buying a pup look into the actual assets and liabilities of his breed *at the present time and under present-day conditions* and let official classifications go hang; not forgetting that your own character and living conditions count. Prime factors you should seriously consider are the following:

1. Your disposition, tastes and favorite recreations. Since dogs are ideal companions it is only common sense to choose your future comrade with an eye to *his* disposition, tastes and favorite recreations. He'll try to make them fit yours whether or no, but why start with a handicap? If you are inclined to be jumpy and sudden and unexpected noises get on your nerves, yet prefer a small dog to a large one, you would surely be better satisfied with a spaniel than with a terrier. Especially if you take a notion to do a little gunning now and then. In the same way any fastidious housewife will tell you white hair is more conspicuous on rugs and furniture than brown or black and that the broom or vacuum cleaner handles short hair better than long.

2. Your occupation. As already said, your dog may be your partner or employee, and a very efficient one, if you read over his references before you take him on. He may drive the cattle to pasture and back to the barn, guard the merchandise you leave in your car when you go into a house, store or factory to make a sale, be your night watchman or burglar alarm or even your nursemaid when you run across the street to borrow a loaf of bread. These services are just a sample.

3. The size and make-up of your family. Some breeds are much better suited to become playmates and protectors of children than certain other

breeds. With the boos of their sponsors ringing in my ears, I'm still brash enough to claim that chow chows, Doberman pinschers, boxers, Siberian huskies and several other breeds are not, as a rule, ideal for this purpose.

4. The state of your health and any infirmities you may have. The fact that some breeds are comparatively hard to handle and their training may require considerable physical strength makes them impractical for certain people. Before you buy a very young puppy of a breed of this kind, picture him as a full-grown dog weighing 140 pounds or more and with muscles of tempered steel.

5. Your bank account. I'll simply call to your attention a daily diet suggested by an eminent veterinary as sufficient for a very large dog eleven months old:

"Morning: One quart of milk, two eggs, three or four pieces of toast or stale bread. Evening: Three to three and a half pounds of chopped beef, three or four cups of cooked vegetables, and half a dozen pieces of whole-wheat bread."

I'm submitting this as Exhibit A and consider it excellent and conservative. But I'm glad I'm not paying that dog's board bill.

Another financial factor is the expense usually incurred in the stripping, plucking or trimming some breeds require if they are to look the part of purebreds instead of unfortunate accidents. Airedale, Bedlington, Kerry Blue, Sealyham, Scottish, Welsh and wire-haired fox terriers, as well as schnauzers and Brussels griffons, are in this class. As for that Beau Brummel of the whole dog family, the poodle, if you wish him to be really *de rigueur,* you should call in a landscape gardener.

Of course you may have the time, patience and skill to give some or all of these beauty treatments yourself. If so, well and good. Otherwise consider the cost.

Short-haired dogs naturally run up no bills at barber or beauty shops, and the same is true of all the sporting dogs, short-haired or otherwise. A thorough brushing and combing every few days makes even the silky little spaniels look well-dressed. This goes for various other long-haired breeds in the list.

6. Where you live. Great Danes, Saint Bernards and Newfoundlands are grand dogs, but out of place in a city apartment — not on account of their dispositions, for they are much less active and quite as good-natured as some of the smaller breeds; but solely on account of their size. All the really big dogs should live as country squires, not men about town; and this applies to the more active medium-sized breeds as well. To confine

dogs of this type to even the most luxurious of city lodgings, limiting their exercise to runs in the park, is not giving them a fair deal.

This statement puts me out on a limb, because Dr. James R. Kinney, Chief Veterinarian at the Ellin Prince Speyer Hospital, and an outstanding authority, says that, in his opinion, city dogs lead healthier and happier lives than many country dogs. Also that investigations by the American Veterinary Medical Association have proved that not only is the city dog healthy, but he lives on the average two or three years longer than the country dog. His explanation is that city owners must be ardent dog lovers or they would not burden themselves with the care of a dog in a place so inherently inconvenient.

In all this Dr. Kinney is undoubtedly correct, but maybe I'm not so far out on that limb as I thought. The very fact that it is so "inherently inconvenient" to take care of any kind of dog in the city is, I think, a mighty sound reason why the city dweller should make that inconvenience as slight as possible by sticking to comparatively small dogs. Yet I must admit there are exceptions. I know quite a few such cases myself, but as it happens there's a catch in each of them. One friend, for instance, keeps a massive Irish Wolfhound in his New York penthouse for days at a time, and the dog is always in excellent health.

But it is significant that this same man owns an extensive estate on Long Island and spends a great deal of his time there. If that were not the case I doubt if the dog could be kept in A-1 condition for long.

7. The perennial (in this case semi-perennial) problem of sex. Here again it all depends on your situation and surroundings, your plans for the future and the breed you select. Males are more subject to wanderlust than females, which are home bodies as a rule. To offset this, for at least two weeks each half-year your female must be kept in close confinement, and it can't be too close or too confining. One little lapse in your vigilance and you are pretty sure to wake up some fine morning to find yourself with a litter of nine or ten question marks on your hands.

Of course this consummation, devoutly to be shunned, may be avoided by the minor operation called "spaying," which any veterinarian will perform for a reasonable fee. But don't have it done unless your living conditions make it imperative, and under no circumstances before your puppy is eight or nine months old. Otherwise it may materially lessen her ambition, spirit and activity and tend to make her lazy and fat.

If you plan to raise puppies later on, this operation is naturally out of the question. Whatever your plans, it's worth remembering that, when the twice-a-year periods occur, small dogs are kept in confinement and under control much more easily, and, in the city, more humanely, than big ones.

Females are sometimes more affectionate than males, fully as intelligent and inclined to be more cleanly in their habits. As might be expected, they are as a rule more sensitive to rebuke or discipline and for that reason easily taught or trained. But they are far more jealous of each other than males and not a bit backward about showing it. If you keep more than one in the same enclosure, stand by for squalls.

To sum it all up, misfits in dogs, as in shoes or evening gowns, are both annoying and unnecessary. But dogs sometimes fail to conform to the specifications laid down for the breed to which they belong. Individuals in breeds that are supposed to be even-tempered may be touchy and others supposed to be bold may be shy. This goes for both mental and physical traits, and makes helping you pick the particular dog of your dreams important enough to deserve a chapter all its own.

CHAPTER IV

Picking Your Pup

SHOPPING for a puppy presents a number of problems, the first of which is where to do it. While many pet shops are thoroughly reliable, it is wiser, if convenient, to deal with a kennel specializing in the breed you have in mind or with an individual breeder whose honesty you have checked and double checked. As a general thing either is as interested in selling you a high-class puppy as you are in buying it. The chances are, the puppies they show you will all be good typical specimens, but to a dog man's expert eye no two are equally desirable, and you can't expect a professional breeder to offer a perfect stranger the best pup in a litter. This means you will probably be asked to make your own selection from six or eight, all of which look confusingly alike. To make the choice still more difficult the individual pups in a litter change from week to week in such a way that the best-looking today may be third best a month from now, and in another four weeks you'll find him back in first place again. This is too tough a nut for even the cleverest novice to crack. The breeder's ace in the hole is the fact that he studied each carefully as soon as it was born and before it had a chance to dry; which is the very best time to determine how it will be put together when it grows up.

In spite of which there are certain externals even a novice can spot. In nearly all breeds look

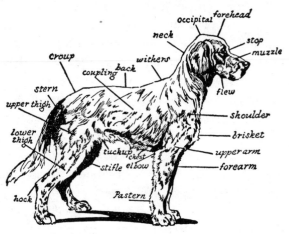

BASIC POINTS TO EXAMINE IN A DOG OR PUP

for dark eyes, small feet with well-arched toes set closely together, well-sprung ribs that give plenty of lung room, good bone well covered with muscle, and the proper breed expression and coat color. This last, of course, may be quite different from that of the same pup when he's a year old; but you should find out what is considered correct for his age.

While all these physical characteristics may indicate a possible bench-show winner later on, there are others more important to the average buyer. Among these are good health, intelligence and the proper disposition. I use "proper" instead of "good" because in certain breeds, such as some of the terriers, a little touchiness of temper is considered desirable. In general, however, the better the disposition the better the dog.

Whatever the breed, choose an active pup that shows no lameness, no malformation of joints, no suggestion of skin disease and no twitching muscles that may indicate chorea. Ask if he has had distemper. If he has and has come through with no aftereffects, so much the better. It's a hundred to one he'll never have it again.

Watch for a pup that responds quickly when spoken to, without a sign of timidity. But don't be bluffed by his apparent self-confidence in his own home yard and among his four-legged playmates. Get him out by himself and watch his reactions to you, a stranger. At the same time don't forget he's a baby and has babyish ways. If he turns over on his back, paws in air, when you go up to him, that doesn't necessarily mean he's shy. Grown dogs that are bold as brass will sometimes do the same when they feel playful. Even crawling isn't a sure sign of shyness. Dogs and pups often crawl simply to express their pleasure. But one thing a timid pup almost never does — chase after you when you turn and walk or run away. Try it and see how your prospective purchase behaves. He may not follow you even if he is not a particle shy, but he will usually act as if he were going to. When all is said and done, your own common sense is the best guide. You know a timid child when you see one; you should be able to spot a timid pup. When you do, forget all his other good qualities and don't buy him. I can't make this too emphatic.

All these directions imply that you have some slight knowledge of dogs; BUT (and the capitals mean what they say) whatever you do, don't try to convey the impression you consider it more than slight. If you do, even a square-shooting breeder will take you at your word, match his wits against yours and suffer no qualms of conscience as he "gives you the works."

After looking over a litter, for example, you are pretty sure to ask if the breeder has anything else in his kennels that might interest you. If your attitude is that of self-considered expert, Mr. Breeder hesitates and studies his boots reflectively.

"Well, yes and no. I've got another one of this same lot that I was figuring on keeping for myself, but if you're willing to pay the price, I suppose I might let him go."

Naturally you ask to see this paragon and ten

minutes later you drive away, the proud possessor of the poorest pup of them all, and for that reason the one the dealer is most anxious to be rid of. As soon as you are out of sight he puts the next poorest in the same state of impressive isolation and the trap is baited for the next cocksure customer.

Another tip: if you drive or ride in a high-priced car, leave it where it can't be seen from the kennels and walk the rest of the way. If you're wearing an old suit of clothes, so much the better. A shining limousine, a liveried chauffeur and a prospective buyer in a suit that cost a hundred and a quarter can boost the price of a mediocre puppy to an amazing figure. The following incident, scrupulously faithful to the facts, illustrates the principle involved.

A friend of mine, now dead and gone and whom I shall call Mr. X, was a good conscientious dog man and an equally good sizer-upper of human nature. One evening he answered the telephone to find Mrs. So-and-So on the wire. He didn't recognize the name, but the address was an ultra-smart hotel. Could he sell her a nice Scottie pup about three months old? The answer was "Yes," the price was $75 and he would bring the pup to her hotel in the morning for inspection.

Two minutes after the lady had hung up, X suddenly realized Mrs. So-and-So was none other than Evelyn Whoosis, glamorous screen star, and So-and-So an equally well-known hero of the films. Also that $75 was much too low a figure to impress either celebrity. So he was glum as a gargoyle next morning when he went out to the kennels to get the pup.

But fate was with him. Before he started for the hotel, So-and-So called up, very evidently suffering from a bad case of temperament. His wife was all wet on that pup proposition, he said. She was a dumbbell about dogs, but he knew all the answers. They didn't want any three-months-old pup; six months was minimum. How about it?

Was X relieved? He was — and then some. He had two really fine six-months-old puppies he was holding at $150 each, but this was his chance to crash the real-money zone. He took them to the hotel, gave the couple a convincing sales talk and finished with the prices. One was $500, the other $750. The movie hero rubbed his chin reflectively.

"Hm. I see. What's the difference between the two?"

There wasn't any difference to amount to anything — it was just a matter of individual preference. X was no liar. He gave So-and-So the gospel truth.

"I just *told* you the difference," he said. "This one is five hundred and that one is seven-fifty."

So-and-So stood off and studied the two dogs

with what he considered the proper professional squint.

"Sure!" he agreed. "I get it now." Then, with easy assurance, to impress the little lady at his side, "There's nothing to it when you know 'em, dear. We'll take this one." And he indicated the $750 pup.

"What was I to do?" X asked me later. "If I had priced that Scottie at what I considered him actually worth those big shots would have figured he was just a mutt, gone somewhere else and taken a *regular* trimming. As it is they've got a real nice dog, even if they did pay an extra six hundred for the satisfaction of showing off."

Then there was the *grande dame* who turned up her nose at a trappy little wire-haired fox terrier at $100, but fifteen minutes later fell for the very same dog, hook, line and lorgnette, when he set her back $400. The breeder simply spent the fifteen minutes giving milady the one-I'm-saving-for-myself yarn, while his kennel man gave the dog an expert once-over with stripping comb, scissors and wire brush, with a deft dusting of white chalk as a finisher. Brought out for the second time, the appearance of the terrier was so changed that milady never suspected a thing, and when she heard the price went into raptures. She simply *had* to have that *wonderful* four-hundred-dollar puppy!

Exceptional cases? Of course. But the country is

full of people who like to pay big prices for dogs (or any other kind of livestock) and judge their quality by the size of the check. You can't blame dog dealers for answering the door when Opportunity knocks with that kind of money in his fist.

While we're on this general subject, there's a popular misconception that deserves a line or two — the blue-ribbon complex. Breeders and dealers know all about it and often persuade a naïve customer to buy a certain pup on the ground that its sire or dam or both won a blue ribbon or two at the shows. It's probably unnecessary to tell you such sales talk is often pure poppycock. All that's necessary to win a blue ribbon is to own a pure-bred dog, enter him in small shows — and keep trying. Sooner or later the dog will be lucky enough to be the only entry in one of the so-called "regular" classes (Puppy, Novice, Limit, American-Bred and Open) — and there's your blue ribbon. Ask your dealer to show you the purple, blue-and-white or purple-and-gold ribbon or rosette his dog has won in the classes named Winners, Best of Winners and Best of Breed. This is not saying all blue ribbons are jokes. A blue at one of the big shows may mean more than a purple at Podunk.

That's about all, and I'll admit it isn't much. To pull it together a bit, here's the advice. Go to a reliable breeder or dealer to get the best you can for your money. Look for a bright, active, good-natured, healthy fellow that isn't afraid to come to you when you call him. When you get your hands on him, go over him for dark eyes, small, well-arched feet with tight toes, well-sprung ribs, good bone, enough muscle for a puppy, and the correct breed expression and coat color. Carry a bit of meat or other morsel in your pocket to test his sense of smell. But beware! A young puppy, even the veriest mutt, is a supersalesman for himself. Once he's in your arms, he'll make you like him whether or no. Steel yourself against his blandishments and resist the temptation to buy a fascinating little rascal simply because he *is* fascinating. He may turn out to be anything but fascinating when he grows up. So study that family tree.

If all these directions seem too formidable to follow, you might as well throw yourself on the mercy of the breeder, tell him what you want and why, and let him fill the order for you. In many cases you might go farther and fare worse.

The price to pay? I throw up my hands. Seventy-five dollars should be tops for a first-class puppy of any of the better-known breeds at three months of age, and $50 is average. And the low? I'll paraphrase the historic reply to Queen Victoria when she asked what was second to the *America* as the Yankee boat swept across the finish line to win that famous cup. I'll simply say: "There *is* no low, Your Majesty."

In case you are buying a grown dog instead of a puppy, the official standard drawn up for the breed to which it belongs is well worth studying, and may be obtained from the American Kennel Club, 221 Fourth Avenue, New York City. While these standards are none too clear to a beginner, they point out fundamentals to look for and glaring defects to avoid. It is still more satisfactory to locate any first-class specimens owned in your vicinity and to fix firmly in your mind their general appearance and characteristics. Better yet, go to a few dog shows and make good use of your eyes and ears and your ability to ask questions.

One final word of warning. Whether you're buying a grown dog or a puppy, don't be put off with a written, typed or printed pedigree showing the ancestry of your prospective purchase for three or four generations. It is too easily faked. Insist on the official application form required for registry in the American Kennel Club Studbook or the Field Dog Studbook, as the case may be, and see that it is signed by the breeder and, in certain cases, by the owner of the sire as well. You may wish to go still further and have this form checked and verified by the organization that issues it before paying your money and taking your dog. If there are irregularities they will be discovered and rectified, usually at no expense to you other than car or bus fare or the price of a postage stamp or two.

Perhaps you'll decide to sidestep all these "dos" and "don'ts" and simply answer an advertisement. If you do, insist that your dog or puppy be sent on approval; that is, that you have the right to inspect it before closing the bargain by paying the C.O.D. charges. This may give you a chance to call in a friend or neighbor who knows more about dogs than you do, and benefit by his advice. I remember a beginner who tried that system, and for $35 and express charges became the owner of a puppy that was the winning female of her breed at Madison Square Garden the following February and a full-fledged champion before the end of the year. This happened fifteen years ago and was so exceptional it has never been forgotten.

CHAPTER V

"Welcome, Stranger"

You are now the owner of your first dog, and unless you are an unusual person, his arrival is a real event. But it is a much greater event in the life of your puppy. Whatever happens, your personality and character will remain about what they always have been and always will be. Jock's entire disposition and behavior will be colored by his association with you and your household.

He will probably arrive in one of three ways: you will bring him home yourself, he will be delivered at your door by his breeder or an employee, or he will be shipped to you and come in a crate.

If you bring him in your automobile he is practically sure to be car-sick. In a few weeks he will consider a motor ride the acme of bliss, but this first experience is physical and mental misery, and almost as distressing to you. Without going into painful details, two or three empty gunnysacks or a few newspapers on the seat and floor of your sedan or roadster, with frequent stops during the trip, will save wear and tear on both your car and your peace of mind. Maybe you will have no trouble at all. The best insurance against sickness is to make sure the pup has had nothing to eat for some time before you start.

A more important reason for bringing Jock to his new home hungry is the fact that a dish of bread and milk and a little chopped meat as soon after his arrival as he feels hungry again will taste like the nectar of the gods. This is why you, as his future teacher and trainer, are the one to give it to him, which is equally true, of course, by whatever method he makes his appearance. Should it be after a long, terrifying trip by rail, it is especially important that you be the one to open his crate and give him his liberty as well as his dinner. That may mean he must wait for hours. Very well; let him wait. He'll never forget your kindness and will try to repay you for it later on by always doing his level best to please you. This will come in mighty handy when you and Jock begin your training sessions by and by. In fact, opening the crate and serving the bewildered little pup that first meal may actually be made the first of those training sessions. On the closing pages of this chapter we'll find out how.

If possible, keep on giving him his meals every day, but that's not 100 per cent essential. Contrary to popular belief, the way to a dog's heart is not necessarily through his stomach. He confers the title of Master on the member of the family who shows him the most attention and gives him the most care. Remember and take full advantage of this trait.

I called your puppy "Jock" just now because he should be christened before or immediately after his arrival and you should at once begin teaching him to recognize and answer to his name. This is just as necessary if he is your only dog as it would be if you owned a dozen. Make the name a word of one syllable, even if, as a registered blue-blood, his moniker of record consists of all three words or the entire twenty-five letters which are the limits officially allowed.

Have a collar and leash in readiness. Jock can't begin too soon to learn the functions of both. The so-called "slip-over" leash costs but a shade more than the ordinary snap-on-the-collar type, and is vastly preferable. For whistling purposes, if you're a good reliable whistler (I don't mean a fancy one), use your lips. If, as in my own case, you're anything but, a well-made metal or wooden whistle should be instantly available whenever you and your pup are in each other's company. Or you might like to experiment with the comparatively new "soundless" whistle called the "Acme," and sold by sporting-goods dealers in the larger cities. The pitch of this ingenious little invention is so high that it fails to register properly on the human eardrum, yet is readily heard and recognized by a dog. Opinions as to its practical value differ, but it is yours for less than $2.00 if you care to call your wandering pup without attracting undue attention elsewhere. Whatever you use, stick to one whistle and one way of blowing it for any given purpose. Handlers of bird dogs in field trials sometimes have a regular code of signals, such as a rapid succession of staccatos to attract the dog's attention when necessary, one long sustained blast as a command to come in to heel, any ordinary blowing of the whistle to send the dog farther out on the course, and so on. You may find a similar system useful in giving any specific orders you may select.

The collar, leash, whistle and a good dog brush, usually a combination of bristles and wire, are all the accessories you will need for some time, so we'll turn to what our grandfathers and grandmothers used to call "bed and board."

If Jock is to stay in your house or apartment at night, provide him with a good bed — and good doesn't mean luxurious. Dogs can sleep comfortably on a bare board floor, provided they are warm enough and not in a direct draft; but for your sake as well as his, the pup should have a regular sleeping place and you should see that he uses it. This may be anything from a piece of old carpeting on the kitchen or laundry floor to a beautiful satin cushion with tassels at each corner and the name "Jock" embroidered in the center, and which occupies a prominent position on the Oriental rug in your boudoir. But I might as well confess here and now that I have two pet aversions: over-petting and pampering dogs, and using baby talk when speaking to them. Pampered dogs become delicate and subject to all kinds of ills just as pampered people do. As for baby talk, it reflects on the intelligence of both you and your puppy. Dogs respect people who are kind but firm, not those who coddle, indulge and spoil them. And mutual respect, as we shall learn a little later, is the very first requirement for establishing ideal relations between you and your dog.

The same principles apply if Jock sleeps in the stable or garage or has bachelor lodgings all to himself in the back yard. If he sleeps outdoors, his house may be anything from an old barrel set on its side to an elaborate kennel. In cold weather hang a gunnysack or, if you insist, a yard of rare Gobelin tapestry at the entrance to keep out cold or drafts. The material you use, like your choice between barrel or kennel, is entirely a matter of your own personal preference, and doesn't mean a thing to Jock. A doghouse, rough or neat and trim, a simple doghouse is to him — and nothing more.

Outdoor quarters, however, have one great advantage. They allow the use of cedar shavings for bedding. Fleas, notoriously democratic and anything but finicky as a rule, simply detest the odor of cedar shavings, possibly because it gives them a headache. The cedar also tends to kill any "doggy" odor your pup may acquire later on. Sleeping in warm rooms, too dry a skin, or poor physical condition may cause this odor. In case the shavings are not practical for you, one or two drops of pine oil on the brush you use religiously every day will keep Jock sweet as well as clean. Don't resort to washing unless you feel it absolutely necessary, and then seldom. Once every two months is often enough, three months is better and six months better yet. Soap and water remove the natural oil in the skin and make it dry and itchy. Sometimes you think it's a flea that's bothering your pup when in reality it's that last tub. Certain breeds, like the retrievers, have a heavy undercoat that keeps water from reaching the skin at all. They are regular ducks for water and it's good for them. If you own that kind of dog you will never have to give him a bath — he'll take it every time he has a chance.

So much for the bed question. Now for board, which is not quite so simple but nothing to be worried about. There are all sorts of scientifically compounded diets for all sorts of dogs. Your veterinary will suggest any or all of them, and they are perfectly reliable of course. As I'm no veterinary, forgive me if I confine myself to a few generalities, the result of experience rather than scientific research.

If you have a very small family or no family at all, you may be obliged to buy food especially for your one lone dog. A fair-sized household, on the contrary, with a collective appetite reasonably normal, will usually supply enough leftovers and table scraps for a small or medium-sized dog; and the variety these everyday dishes offer will keep him as fit as if you could count every calorie in every meal.

Naturally there are a few fundamentals for proper feeding that every dog owner should know. The best and most easily understood rule for grown dogs is two thirds meat in every meal, and between meals large bones to gnaw on. Any meat except pork or pork products is all right, and, in my experience, there's nothing radically wrong about even a pork chop now and then. In vegetables almost anything except the starchy and sugary kinds, like potatoes, beans and beets will do. Of the fruits, bananas are supposed to be bad. Meat and vegetable soups are always excellent and easy to provide. Commercial prepared foods with trade names are good or otherwise according to brand. You'd best consult your veterinary before buying in wholesale lots. Bread, even though starchy, is allowed by A-1 veterinaries in reasonable quantities.

"Large bones to gnaw on" means large bones to gnaw on. Chicken and fish bones are not large and dogs don't gnaw them — they chew them a second or two, then swallow them — or don't swallow them. If they do swallow them the gastric juice in a dog's stomach is so extremely efficient it reduces almost anything to jelly in a comparatively few minutes. If they do not swallow them it's because they can't. Fish and chicken bones splinter very easily and sometimes the sharp points pierce a dog's gullet and stick there, which is serious. So — "only large bones to gnaw on."

For nearly all grown dogs one square meal a day is enough and it should be served in the early evening. The average house dog eats too much, not too little. If Jock happens to be choosy about his food, you can readily find out what he likes and dislikes and cater to him a trifle. But when he gulps down a good big dinner as if he were starving to death, then pleads pathetically for more, don't let him fool you. Nearly all dogs eat that way and plead that way. It's a combination of instinct and Machiavellian guile, and should be taken for what it's worth — which is exactly nothing at all.

These "chef's suggestions," such as they are, are for grown dogs. For a few months you will be more interested in how and what to feed your growing puppy. Give him four meals a day until he is nearly six months old; then drop to three until he is about eleven months, and from then on he should have only one, or in certain cases two, according to his size, appetite and condition.

For a two-months-old pup begin with a cup of milk or a saucer of bread and milk in the early morning; follow this about 10 A.M. with a little meat, chopped very fine. Dinner, served about six, might consist of chopped meat and vegetables. This is followed by a before-going-to-bed cup of milk. There is nothing hard-and-fast about this, understand. Every dog and every pup is a law unto himself. Your common sense and Jock's stomach should be able to settle it between them; and from the time the pup is three months old until he's a grown dog you will gradually increase the amount he is allowed to eat and what it consists of to suit his taste and your convenience. A tea-spoonful of cod-liver oil mixed with Jock's dinner every few days will help things along, and a very small bit of garlic cut very fine and mixed with the same meal is not only a grand conditioner but one of the very best preventives of worms. The chopped meat referred to may be either cooked or raw. If its source was leftovers and table scraps, it will probably be cooked. Incidentally most dogs like it better that way, at least until they become used to the raw material, and as far as I know, it does them just as much good.

But we should be leaving all these inanimate things like dog collars, dog leashes, doghouses and dog foods and getting back to dogs themselves, which are animate enough to suit the most exacting, and for that reason much more interesting. And while we're still on the subject of food and feeding, it's a good time to mention the fairly common custom of allowing your dog to sit by your table while you're at a meal so that you can toss choice morsels for him to catch. There's no law against it, not even a social one as far as I know, so you may jolly well do as you please about it; but to me it's a poor practice for a number of reasons. For one thing, it makes for a messy floor. For another, an eager dog may easily do a lot of damage around a dining table, if it's only to hit your elbow with his nose and make you spill your coffee on a lace doily or linen tablecloth. Third and most important, *you* may enjoy having your dog grab and gobble a piece of meat caught on the fly, but what is meat to you and Jock may be poison to any guests you may have. If they dislike dogs it may ruin their whole meal, and even if they like dogs, watching your pet "wolf down" his food may be anything but appetizing.

Now that all these gustatory rules and regulations, diets, etc., etc., are disposed of, you may remember you were just about to give Jock his first meal at his new home and that I said it could be made the first step, and a very important one, in his training. That wasn't very clear, so I'll explain.

As everyone knows, instant obedience to the voice and whistle is the cornerstone of the whole educational structure. All sorts of more or less mechanical methods have been used to lay this cornerstone, but in my opinion it is most easily and effectively done if you use a feed pan for a trowel, a good meal for mortar and your voice and whistle as the vocal and instrumental part of the ceremony. Jock must be taught to consider your whistle or the command "Jock! Come here!" as irresistible as the flute of the Pied Piper of Hamelin. He *will* consider it so for the time being if you whistle to him or repeat that command several times as you give him that first dinner; and he will keep right on considering it so if you do the same thing every time you feed him. Do it two or three times as he watches you cut up his meat and vegetables, do it again when you set them before him and stand by for an occasional repeat as he stows them away. And don't confine this to mealtimes. Whistle or call now and then whenever you and Jock are out for a walk, always having a tiny tidbit in your pocket to give him when he comes to you promptly. Before he realizes it, instant obedience will become a fixed habit. From then on no tidbit will be necessary. Jock will obey **the summons** because he can't help it — he doesn't know why, but he can't — and his education will be off to a flying start. A pup that will come to you instantly when you whistle or call is under control at all times; and control at all times is the answer to a trainer's prayer.

CHAPTER VI

The Housebreaking Bugaboo

By noon on the day following his arrival, Jock will probably be pretty much at home and consider himself a full-fledged member of the family. You're lucky if he didn't oblige with a concerto in E minor during most or all of his first night away from his mother and his brothers and sisters. But if you left him severely alone to discover his plaintive notes brought no one to sympathize with him, the chances are it will be his last recital of that kind. Once he's up and about, his day will be a busy and happy one.

You are pleased to find he is already learning to recognize his name when he hears it, and possibly even comes to you now and then when you whistle or call.

In this connection, and much to your amusement, he scrambles up and down stairs as if he had been brought up in a lighthouse. Yet we repeatedly read detailed directions for teaching pups to do this very simple thing. That, I'm afraid, is educational window-dressing. Unless your pup is suffering from mental or physical paralysis he'll learn the trick the first time he finds it useful or even interesting. My latest acquisition in the pup line mastered this supposedly difficult stunt in exactly six minutes flat. All the training he got from me consisted in my walking up and down with him; yet at the end of the six minutes I had to hustle to keep on even terms when going in either direction. Since this pup has long since proved himself no canine Einstein you may be pretty sure Jock will do as well.

As a matter of fact, walking up and down stairs with your pup, as I did, you will probably find quite unnecessary. The sure-fire way to teach a young and active pup to climb stairs is to leave him on the first floor, confident he will be unable to get to the second floor; then go into your second-floor den and try to concentrate on an important job of reading, writing or whatnot. The pup will be biting at your shoelaces or chewing the fringe off the table cover in something like two and a half minutes. To teach him to come down instead of up, you simply leave him upstairs and try to do your concentrating in some room on the ground floor. In my experience, it's as simple — and exasperating — as that!

To come back to general conditions, it is an interesting day for you both. Playing with Jock is as amusing to you as it is to him, for you get almost as big a kick out of giving him his dinner as he does out of eating it and find he enjoys having you brush and comb that funny puppy coat of his as much as or more than you do. All in all, everything seems to be going famously.

Everything — with one tragic exception. A half hour after you first took Jock into the house the chances are you discovered in an out-of-the-way corner in the library something which you hoped against hope you might be spared — that nightmare, and daymare too, the housebreaking problem. I use the word "chances" because Jock may be one of those exceptionally exceptional pups so naturally fastidious that they require no housebreaking at all, in which case you simply bestow a superior smile on the world and everybody and everything in it and turn to the next chapter.

This does not mean that dogs are by nature untidy in this respect. Even puppies prefer clean quarters to filthy ones. If Jock sleeps in an outdoor kennel and his chain is of reasonable length, he will seldom soil the shavings, straw or even earth inside. He will choose as his "rest room" a spot as far away from his bedroom as the length of his chain will allow. What he doesn't understand is that *you* are even more particular about *your* house; and it's your business to teach him that little lesson as quickly as you can.

You can step this up by following a few rules, no one of which is directly corrective *per se,* but all of which put together will help things along.

1. If Jock's bed is in your house or if he spends much of his time indoors, for the first few weeks confine him strictly to one room, preferably the kitchen or laundry, which presumably has washable floors. This makes it comparatively easy to keep an eye on him, anticipate accidents and put him outdoors before they occur. Even when they do happen, an old mop, plied with much, little or no profanity, will repair the damage.

2. Feed your pup at the same hours each day. If he gets his food regularly he will be pretty sure to get rid of waste material regularly, too. When you have learned the usual interval between a meal and its natural result, you can take the pup out of the house a little before the clock strikes.

3. Young puppies are inveterate and even intemperate water drinkers. If water is available at all times they will swill down much more than is good for them and become actually waterlogged. This increases their demands on your time and attention. Give Jock water after each meal; at other times only when he asks for it. He'll learn the purpose of the faucet in the kitchen sink in no time and if he's really thirsty his actions will speak louder than words.

4. If you live in the country or suburbs let Jock out for a run as soon as you are out of bed in the morning. Do this regularly and he will probably

take the hint. But watch him from your window to make sure. There is now and then an unregenerate rascal who will gambol on the green for a full half hour, only to use the kitchen linoleum a minute and a half after he is indoors again. We shall consider this fellow in a page or two.

Such solo runs before breakfast are practically impossible in the city, where there is usually an ordinance to the effect that a dog is not to appear on the street without his leash, and that his leash must have somebody at the other end of it. Taking a constitutional before breakfast may be healthy, but most of us would rather pass it up and take a digestive tablet instead. If that is your attitude, get a wooden or corrugated-paper box large enough for Jock to turn around in and strong enough to last two or three weeks, cover the bottom with a layer of paper cuttings and put it in an accessible place in the kitchen or laundry. Teach Jock to use it by putting him in it when he flies storm signals, or, in case you're not quick enough, immediately after you realize you are too late. A few old newspapers on the floor may take the place of the box, but they are less satisfactory because easily disarranged and scattered about. Renew the cuttings or newspapers every morning, but always leave a little slightly soiled paper as a reminder. Dogs use their noses for brains in many cases, and this happens to be one of them.

NOTICE! IMPORTANT! Pat and praise Jock when he voluntarily makes use of the box or papers. Scold him with a warning "No! No!" when you find yourself an accessory *after* instead of *before* the fact. If he is exceptionally obstinate about taking your tip, don't take any back talk. Wait till you catch him in the act, whip him with a folded newspaper, scold him roundly with plenty of "No, no's" and dump him unceremoniously into his box. Let the dumping be as rough as his constitution will stand and make him stay in the box until he has had ample time to think things over.

This doesn't mean you should lose your temper. You may *hurt* Jock a little without doing him a particle of harm, but to *frighten* him is fatal. Even after a good stiff whipping, a pup or grown dog can think things over and draw logical conclusions from his unpleasant experience, but only provided you use self-control when you use the folded paper or switch. Violent exhibitions of anger are terrifying, and he will be in a hopeless mental tailspin when hurt and frightened at the same time.

A friend of mine, an important executive in a big corporation, told me one day: "In dealing with employees I never lose my temper unless I've thought it all over beforehand and decided it's the smart thing to do." Meaning, of course, he never loses his temper at all; he simply pretends to lose it when he feels such synthetic anger wise.

Once in an exceptionally blue moon this system may work in dealing with a cunning old dog that disobeys purposely, just for the hell of it; but with a puppy or young dog, never. Don't even *pretend* to lose your self-control.

You realize, I'm sure, that the box-and-paper system is positive training and you will probably

CORRECT WAY TO PUNISH
A DOG

make use of it whether you pay your dog tax in New York City or Noodlebury Center; also that it is an all-day proposition, whenever the pup is in the house, not simply a "morning glory."

The outdoor program is comparatively simple. You already know about that run after Jock has finished each meal. During this little outing he may be expected to take advantage of the various opportunities offered, but make sure he keeps away from valuable shrubs or flowers in private grounds or public parks. You can buy commercial preparations to spray on your own delicate plants and shrubs to protect them from Jock's sprinkling proclivities. If possible see to it he isn't forced to resort to paved streets, and under no circumstances allow him to make a public nuisance of himself by using a sidewalk. All other considerations aside, neither paved street nor sidewalk is attractive to a dog unless other dogs have used it, and what's even more important from a housebreaking angle, both are too much like your kitchen floor to be educational.

Another tip: make it a practice to take Jock over the same route on each trip of this kind. Dogs have their favorite comfort stations, and the regular use of certain rocks, bushes, trees, and so forth, readily becomes a habit. Remember, however, what we said just now about avoiding delicate shrubs, plants and flowers in private grounds or public parks. Try to select an itinerary that offers few, if any, opportunities for that kind of vandalism, not only because it *is* vandalism, but also because it's a bad idea to watch the pup too closely as he noses about. This may sound silly, but believe it or not, dogs have a certain sense of modesty, self-consciousness or whatever you care to call it, and it's a good idea to play up to it. Whenever the use of a suitable rock, tree or bush seems likely, appear utterly uninterested in your pup and intensely interested in something else.

In a few months, when Jock has learned the purpose of his romp, you may forget this advice and even suggest that he hurry up and get it over with; but it's only natural a young pup should be a trifle furtive. He has usually been punished

WRONG WAY TO PUNISH A DOG

for infractions of the rules inside the house and is not yet quite sure the same regulations are not in force outdoors. Incidentally, if your neighbor will lend you his well-broken dog or he and his dog will join you and Jock to make it a foursome, you will find the dog next door a far better teacher than you are. Pups are notorious imitators.

To return now to that unregenerate pup who considers his early morning run a preliminary workout for serious business as soon as he's back in the house again, these walks we've been talking about should settle his case. Stay with him for a few minutes when you return to the house after the first walk or two, and you'll probably catch him in the act. Give him a good tongue-lashing, punish him with a folded newspaper and put him outside again, speeding the parting pest with as many solid slaps as your agility and the pup's speed and dodging ability will permit. Results may be disappointing for a while, but before long the culprit will decide he can sidestep a lot of sore spots and woes by doing his duty in the open air.

When I used the word "slaps" just now I didn't mean slaps with your bare hand, but with the folded newspaper. It's a fundamental principle of training never to use your hand, bare or gloved, to inflict punishment on a dog. Reserve it for the acts the dog enjoys, such as a pat on the head, a friendly slap on the ribs or the offer of that tidbit you will find so useful all through Jock's training. It may be used as a warning sometimes, or as sign language to indicate something you want him to do; but *never to inflict even the slightest* pain. Jock should learn to welcome the touch of your hand, not to fear or distrust it.

Follow all these housebreaking suggestions conscientiously and you will save Jock a good percentage of the punishment he might otherwise receive, and you'll save yourself considerable punishment too.

CHAPTER VII

Short Detour. Do Dogs Reason?

UP TO NOW you and Jock have gotten along pretty comfortably and pleasantly together. What few simple lessons he has learned have not been particularly irksome to him, nor has teaching them been very much trouble to you. You have become fond of each other. Jock knows his name and answers to it, is neat and clean inside the house and easily controlled in that respect when outdoors, has a good healthy appetite, sleeps soundly because he's pup-tired when bedtime comes, and is growing so fast you've already had to let out his collar a notch.

During your first few walks Jock probably didn't take too kindly to being led, but he gave in gracefully enough in a few days probably. He may still do a little pulling and hauling on occasion, but it's much too early to expect perfect manners when on leash. As a matter of fact, to try to make him acquire them now is not only unnecessary but unwise. High spirits in a young puppy should be encouraged, not repressed. When he pulls too hard just give your leash a little good-natured jerk and let it go at that.

He is a very busy individual. The instant he sees anything he has never noticed before, he begins to investigate it with two things in mind — what is it, and how can I have some fun with it? And since, like Oscar Wilde, he can resist anything but temptation, he is not only amusing but often destructive as well. In other words, he is acquiring by the minute bad habits it will take hours to correct.

Knowing, as you do, that good house dogs are largely a manufactured product, you are pretty sure to decide that the manufacturing cannot begin too soon and that it's high time you took Jock's further education in hand. As a general thing this is a mistake. Forcing a young pup is as foolish as forcing a young child. Infant prodigies, whether children or puppies, usually turn out to be disappointments in the end. So wink at Jock's annoying little sins of omission and commission for a while. Be satisfied with the ground he has already gained and bide your time — even if you wait until he is six months old. While you're waiting, we can profitably consider a few interesting angles you should look into before attempting more extended and intensive schooling.

Education, they say, means drawing out, not pouring in; and you can't be expected to draw out the best in Jock's intellectual and emotional make-up unless you have a fairly accurate blueprint of what that best actually is. You will be wasting your time trying to develop his reasoning powers if he has none to develop; and appealing to his desire to please you is ridiculous if no such desire exists. One rule for successful teaching might well be: pigeonhole your pupil before you begin.

This brings up the age-old question: can dogs reason? People who have tried to answer it are divided into two opposing factions. Both agree that dogs *seem* to reason; but Faction A claims this so-called reasoning is nothing more than *applied instinct,* or instinct modified by centuries of domestication. Faction B, now in the majority I think, holds that dogs reason in exactly the same way, but not of course to the same extent, that people do. If you are interested read "Individual Differences in Dogs" by Professor E. G. Sarris of the University of Hamburg, translated by S. Boehm.[1]

Like nearly all students of animal intelligence, Sarris used the appetites of his various canine subjects to get a line on their intelligence. His findings, as summarized by his translator, are as follows:

[1] *American Kennel Gazette,* November 1938 to February 1939.

The sum total of the experiments proves not only the dog's power of reasoning and of drawing conclusions — if circumstances are fitted to its *"Umwelt"* — but it also evidences the sharp differences in the mental equipment of individual animals. The Sarris tests ascertain in a scientific way that there are intelligent dogs and more or less stupid dogs; and that these variations in mentality are very much the same as in human beings.

The word *Umwelt,* according to Mr. Boehm, means "the surrounding world of the dog" or the specific environment in which it lives and which it is capable of understanding.

Professor Sarris' expert testimony must carry great weight; yet it seems to me ordinary everyday experiences and observations should be enough to convince us that numberless dog doings are the result of pure reason. It's the exceptional house dog that fails to surprise the human members of the family by figuring out more or less complex situations that have nothing whatever to do with instinct, and *drawing logical conclusions therefrom.*

Which brings us to another consideration — your pup's *emotional* reactions to you and the schooling he gets.

Assuming you use anything remotely approaching good judgment, these reactions can be predicted with accuracy. Every normal pup's slogan is

"We aim to please," and he lives up to it. If he were able he would bring his teacher a big red apple every time he comes to school, and his desperate efforts to make you realize how much he thinks of you are almost pathetic. Handle him with any sort of common sense, and no amount of annoyance, mystification, weariness or even physical pain can kill his affection. He is scolded, has his ear pinched and his toes trod on, is yanked around with a rope and even punished a little perhaps with a newspaper or leather leash; all during a single half-hour lesson.

Yet he comes back for more the next day as cheerful as ever, and can still sign himself with absolute sincerity: "Your loving pupil, Jock." When you become trainer of a pup, you have from the start what teachers of human children sometimes never gain — the sincere affection of their pupil or pupils. You also have something else almost equally valuable — respect for you and your infallibility so complete and unquestioning it amounts to idolatry. To Jock you are much more than a teacher — you are all-wise and omnipotent — his god or goddess. Never give him cause to question the soundness of that opinion.

CHAPTER VIII

Pigeonholing Your Pupil

I HOPE you are already inclined to agree that dogs have brains somewhat similar to ours and use them in somewhat the same way. Also that their emotions, while fewer and much more simple and primitive, are almost as keenly felt and, we might add, usually more honestly and openly displayed.

We mustn't overestimate the mental equipment of a pup four months of age; but we mustn't underestimate it either. To give the little devils their due, the knowledge of this somewhat intricate world that such babies have picked up during their 120 days on earth is next to incredible. Especially when we consider that for the first 10 of that 120 they were totally blind. But we *don't* consider it; we take their amazing precocity in stride as a matter of course. Incidents like the following, for instance. Except that the two puppies involved were three months old instead of four.

Spick and Span, litter brother and sister, had always been kept in my garage and had never set foot in the house in their lives. One day Spick came running to the side door and barked and scratched at the wire screen until he attracted the attention of the kitchen maid, who was the only one in the house at the time. Spick had never even seen this maid, as far as I know; yet when the woman came to the door to find out what all the fuss was about, he welcomed her with shrill yelps of delight, then led her across the yard into the garage. There she found Span caught through the nostril by a pickerel hook and held fast by its long gut leader, which was hung on a nail.

Span wasn't even crying, just "moanin' low" as she pulled steadily but uselessly to get free. But Spick had sensed the situation and knew it was serious. He also knew *some human being, no matter who,* was the one to turn to for assistance and that *human beings were to be found in houses.* Also that the way to get them out of houses was to go to a door and make a lot of noise. Would a three-year-old child think more clearly and act with better judgment? None that live in my neighborhood.

You can safely credit Jock with a good memory, too, which you will of course use over and over again in his schooling. A short short about Nip, another pup of mine, will serve as proof.

One summer when he was about the age of Spick and Span in that last episode, he used to ride around with my son, then just out of college, in an old Buick runabout. As this antiquated affair was an open job, the boy guarded against Nip's jumping out by slipping the loop end of a short snap-on leash over the gearshift lever.

In the fall my son went to work in the city, and for three years the broken-down old buzz wagon stood forgotten in an out-of-the-way corner in the garage. Meanwhile the leash, a type I never use, hung on a hook gathering dust. But one morning I found I had mislaid my regular slip-over leash and, as I was in a hurry, snapped the short one into Nip's collar. Instantly he began trying to pull me toward the Buick, and, when I humored him, put his front paws on the running board and waited for me to open the door. Meaning that memories of rides he had enjoyed as a puppy of three months came back to him in a split second at the age of three years. If you are also inclined to give him credit for remarkable powers of observation in instantly recognizing the difference between the old leash and the one he usually wore, forget it. It wasn't observation, it was that sensitive nose of his. It was the association of the leash with the Buick that indicated memory.

Yet, with all the intelligence we have been trying to emphasize, neither pups nor grown dogs understand much of what we say to them. But they do understand *certain individual words in almost everything we say to them.* Or perhaps I should put it a little differently: they understand the meaning of certain vowel sounds we use in various combinations with diphthongs to make words. To illustrate, six months from now Jock will probably drop as readily to the command "Drown!" or "Gown!" as he will to "Down!" And he will react just as strongly to the tone and inflection of your voice as to the words you speak. Call him a good-for-nothing little bum in dulcet tones and he'll wriggle with joy. Tell him sharply he's the most wonderful dog in the world and you'll hurt his feelings. So, in giving orders, use as few words as possible and exactly the same word or phrase for any given command. Don't say "Down!" today and "Charge!" tomorrow. Make it a general rule (to which there are exceptions, as in the case of old and well-trained dogs who deliberately disobey) to speak in a firm, quiet voice and don't change your inflection. And don't give him a lesson immediately after he has eaten a hearty meal. Dogs, like people, are inclined to be a bit logy, both mentally and physically, after eating. Then, too, the hungrier Jock is, the more he will look forward to the tidbit you give him when he does as he's told and the more he will appreciate it after he gets it.

Right here we should take up a training fundamental you will hear a good deal about before you finish this book and which is not only vitally important, but to me about the most fascinating subject in dog psychology. For a good many pages we have been stressing the mental and emotional similarities between ourselves and our dogs. There's still another, much more intriguing, I think. As the old-time evangelists used to put it: "We're all poor sinners!"

But human sinners and dog sinners are totally different, and it is this difference you must take into consideration in your efforts to educate Jock from now on. As a matter of fact, most of his sins are not really sins at all, in the sense that yours and mine are; they are merely instinctive acts inspired by inborn habits and traits that not only were perfectly legitimate for dogs in their original wild state; they were absolutely essential to their very existence. Taken together, they formed a code for dog conduct as necessary for their right living as the Ten Commandments are for ours. In other words, in comparing human and canine misdeeds, we shall find the sins themselves may be similar, but the reasons why they are committed are not.

Naturally the jungle code we just mentioned many times runs absolutely counter to our own rules for moral conduct in our highly civilized human society. If I creep up to your bedroom window some night, watch you put a roll of bills in the top drawer of your dresser, wait until you're sound asleep, then break in and make off with the money, I'm a thief and it's barely possible **I** may be caught and punished. When Pat, the Irish terrier, trots up the knoll, catches Buck, the beagle, in the act of burying a bone, sneaks away without being seen, bides his time, then digs up the bone and makes off with it, he is no thief; he's just a smart little dog doing exactly what any other smart little dog would do under the same circumstances.

Yet while implicit obedience to this instinctive code is a cardinal virtue instead of a crime, Jock's affection for you and his determination to please you at any cost will make him willing to scrap practically all his inborn ideology for your sake. So give him a break. Remember he still has his primitive instincts and that they are strong and impelling. Try to find out what they are and be a little charitable toward them, and you will unlock a lot of doors. To put it in words of one syllable, when Jock does wrong it's two to one he thinks he's right. Don't overlook that point when you are obliged to show him he's not.

Now suppose you sit back in your chair, light your briar, cigar or cigarette and try to review what you have already learned about the puzzling little fellow whose main object in life at the moment seems to be to catch a large yellow-and-black butterfly flitting about among your honeysuckles.

Your résumé is probably something like this: you are by now fairly well convinced you have a remarkable animal on your hands, especially for one so young. He not only has a distinct and interesting personality; he is surprisingly intelligent, has an excellent memory, a nose that is going to prove useful in a hundred ways, both to him and to you; and best of all, you are not only the one being in all the world he loves the most, you are also the one he respects most thoroughly and trusts most implicitly. In other words, he has the ideal attitude of pupil toward teacher, an attitude you now highly resolve to foster and cultivate as well as you know how. Add to all this the fact that his moral character, according to dog standards, is almost 100 per cent beyond reproach, and the total is not only impressive, it is also tremendously encouraging. It looks as if you had a star pupil to deal with.

But star pupils are nearly always a challenge first-class teachers recognize and meet with their fingers crossed. In the case of you and Jock, for instance, his affection for you and blind confidence in your infallibility are delicately balanced emotional and mental hurdles it will require more than a little tact and skill to take without an occasional cropper. We'll put it abstractly like this:

Dogs apparently are able to reason. Therefore their trainers can expect them not only to under-

stand and obey any specific and reasonable command, but also to figure out in their very simple
and primitive way why the command was given
and why they should obey it.

Many a wise old dog goes much further than
that. He not only does things he dislikes to do
because he realizes their purpose and value and
because he is commanded by his master to do
them; he often does similarly distasteful things
he knows are important entirely *on his own responsibility without any command whatever*. If
you doubt it, here's a sample.

In sporting parlance, bringing game to hand
after the kill is called "retrieving," as you probably know. Some dogs dislike to do this and, unless
taught by the use of mild force, simply find and
point dead birds which the gunner picks up for
himself. But in the early fall when the foliage is
thick, a hunter frequently fails to realize he has
made a kill, reloads his gun and goes on in search
of other game.

Five times out of ten, when this happens and if
the gunner is shooting over a smart setter or
pointer, he suddenly misses his dog. If he knows
his canine quirks, he will waste no time whistling
or calling; he'll simply sit down, light his pipe
and wait. In a few moments along will come Mr.
Pointer or Setter, the dead bird in his mouth. He
hates retrieving, yes — but when his master's poor

eyesight threatens the loss of a good plump bird, it's another platter of roast grouse, and he throws his objections to the wind.

I remember a little Gordon setter that was never taught to retrieve and hated the taste of woodcock; yet she would invariably swim out and bring to shore such birds as fell in a wide brook or little pond hole in the woods. *But the shore was her limit.* The moment she set foot on land, where she figured her master could pick up the bird as well as she could, she dropped it like a hot potato.

These incidents may not adorn a tale, but they point a moral. Competent trainers will make sure their commands *are* reasonable, and that, if humanly possible, they convince their pupils of the fact. In certain specific cases the trainer can do more than that. He can arrange his routine so cleverly that his pupil trains himself, obeying orders or permanently correcting bad habits on his own initiative, as the pointer and Gordon setter did on very especial occasions only. This may sound like decidedly deep stuff, but in Chapter IX I shall try to demonstrate it is nothing of the kind.

Two Types of Faults and How Each Should Be Handled

WE LEARNED a few minutes ago that all Jock's faults, or nearly all, can be divided into two distinct classes. Twice out of every three times he does wrong he thinks he's doing right, because his instinct tells him so. That's Class Number One. The third time he either knows he's disobeying instructions or strongly suspects he may be doing something wrong, whether he's ever been told so or not. That's Class Number Two. Each class requires totally different treatment, and it is up to you to size up situations as they arise, decide in which class each belongs and make the punishment fit the crime.

As a typical example of Number One, it is Jock's affection and his desire to show it that makes him jump all over you with his muddy paws and send your nice new white flannel trousers or golf skirt to the cleaners. Since he does it from the very best of motives it's only natural he feels both hurt and mystified when you reward him with a scolding and a stinging slap in the face. Of course enough of these scoldings and slaps distributed over a sufficient length of time will cure him of the habit, but the remedy is a dud because it may have several very definite and very unfortunate kickbacks.

Most important of these is that the pup's belief in your godlike infallibility receives a shock. It seems you have eccentricities, just as he has, and decidedly disagreeable ones at that, among which is your surprising aversion to being told he is extremely fond of you. He forgives this because you are still his ideal and can do no wrong, but he is disillusioned, even if only slightly — and that's bad.

But that's not all. You may have remembered what we said about using your hand to inflict pun‧ ishment — that it was entirely wrong in principle — and used a newspaper or perhaps your leash to slap Jock down. Fine — as far as it goes — but it doesn't go far for the reason that the jump-up nuisance is one thing that others besides yourself try to correct, and they are pretty sure to use their hands. Now, since it's inconceivable to Jock that all human beings can have your strange antipathy to his well-meant and, in his opinion, perfectly harmless advances, he tries them on Phyllis Faber, who lives down the block and has run over to show herself in her new powder-blue marquisette, which she rightfully considers *le dernier cri*. To his astonishment and dismay he again gets a whole barrage of scolding and slaps and retreats to the nearest bombproof shelter he can locate, where he sits down to think it over. His conclusions may run something like this:

"Both my master and that Faber girl have a queer streak. I can forgive my master because I know he likes me and because he does so many nice things for me, but I'm off the Faber girl for life."

But he still can't believe all human beings are like that — it doesn't make sense — so he still tries jumping up on everybody he meets, and nine times out of ten gets the same results. That settles it — enough is enough. People aren't the desirable friends and playmates he had thought, and from now on he'll leave them severely alone and try to see to it they leave him alone, too, with the result that before you know it, you may have that abomination of abominations, a man-shy pup. Or if he is not afraid of *people,* he's afraid of their *hands.* This may make you a lot of trouble later on. It gives you the kind of dog that may growl or snap at strangers when they try to pat him. And nine strangers out of every ten will try to do just that.

You will notice I've not said this would necessarily be the outcome — merely that it might be. Whatever happens, the whole scolding-and-slap-

ping program was unwise because you were taking
not only a long chance — but an unnecessary one.
Had you diagnosed the case before you began
treating it, you would have played safe by doing
something like this:

STEPPING ON DOG'S TOES TO
BREAK HIM OF LEAPING ON
YOU WITH MUDDY PAWS

Instead of slapping or even scolding the well-
meaning little fellow, you would have taken his
two muddy forepaws in your two hands to keep
him standing on his hind feet, at the same time
telling him in honeyed tones what a perfect little
angel you thought him. Meanwhile you very
quietly and carefully plant the toe of your leather
shoe on one of his rear feet, bearing down with

as much pressure as you feel his tender toes will stand.

Jock naturally struggles to free his foot, which you allow him to do almost immediately. But he's only a puppy and has a lot to learn about cause and effect. Besides, he was too much interested in you to see the cause; he thinks the pain in his toes the result of some unfortunate accident in no way connected with you, and which in all probability will never occur again. So he repeats his attempt to show his affection by the Johnny-jump-up method. To his astonishment the twinges in his toes are repeated, too. After a few more tries, it dawns on him that the jumps always seem to cause the twinges. He sits down as before to think it over, but this time his conclusions are radically different.

He still believes his way of telling you he loves you is sound in principle because it very evidently pleases you as much as he expected it would. But it's a flat failure in practice. It doesn't pay because it's too painful. When he tries it on other people with similarly unsatisfactory results (which you should see to it he gets) he very sensibly decides to throw the whole idea into the ashcan and figure out some better way, such as looking up into people's faces and wagging his tail furiously. He tries this and it proves an instantaneous success. He gets not only kind words but also a lot of approving pats on the back and rubbing behind the ears, both of which he enjoys immensely. So he makes that his system from now on. But what is far more important to you, he has lost not one iota of confidence in his master, or mistress, or in humans in general, and still considers them as much worth cultivating as he always has.

Sometimes simply holding your pup's paws firmly and backing him slowly while he is on his hind legs is all that is necessary. But don't omit those honeyed words. Like the magician's running fire of patter, they hold Jock's attention as you pull the disciplinary rabbit out of your hat.

You may have noticed that this particular case illustrates two cardinal principles of training instead of one. You were not only perfectly reasonable in making Jock keep off your clean trousers; you did it in such a way that Jock never realized you were making him do *anything,* reasonable or unreasonable. It was one of those rare cases where the pup apparently trains himself and corrects a bad habit on his own initiative. With this routine it was unnecessary to convince Jock your command was reasonable because, as far as he knew, there was no command at all.

So much for a fault in Class One and its correction. Now let's take an example of Class Two, a situation in which Jock knows he's breaking a rule that he has no right to consider unreasonable.

If he is allowed indoors at all he has by this time been permitted to "come out of the kitchen" and join the family in the living room and library, or it may be he has free run of the house. He is quick to realize his good fortune and make the most of it. In less than no time he discovers the big davenport in the living room is the most luxurious lounging place in the house. Also that this is true whether his feet are muddy or clean, wet or dry; and the fact that his wiry white hairs stick to its fine upholstery like burrs is an equally unimportant detail.

He will jump down to the floor when you whistle or call, for by now he obeys either summons instantly; but that's not the answer. Many times there is no one near to do the whistling or calling. He must learn household furniture is for people, not pups, and that this is true at all times, even when he is all sole alone in the house. Keeping his feet on the floor must become a *fixed habit,* as in the case in which your white flannels and Phyllis Faber's powder-blue frock were featured.

The firm "No!" or "No, no!" which you used repeatedly during Jock's housebreaking lessons, and which you will continue to use over and over again for all sorts of reasons for the next few months, is the obvious command to accompany your whistle or voice.

If Jock is the sensitive sort and you and the rest

of your family are persistent in this, it may be all that is necessary. If he's a bold little beggar, which of the two extremes is preferable, don't be afraid to drive him off the davenport with a few sound slaps with a folded newspaper, a stern "No, no!" accompanying each slap. The paper doesn't

CORRECTING DOG OF FAULT
OF JUMPING ON FURNITURE

really hurt but he dislikes it because the *sound* of the blows is unpleasant in itself and ominous because it suggests something much worse.

Even more ominous are the words "No, no!" and the tone of voice you use in speaking them. They show him you are thoroughly displeased and perhaps even disgusted. This is serious. Apparently he is not living up to that slogan of his, "We aim to please." But he's only a youngster.

Maybe his deduction is not correct, so the next time he feels like taking a nap, he selects the sofa again. Again he finds himself either figuratively or literally in the doghouse. This may go on for days, but the minute he's convinced the nap and the scolding and slaps are cause and effect he's cured — as far as the davenport is concerned. But being quite a philosopher in a small way, he decides the big overstuffed easy chair by the window is just as comfortable anyhow. When he finds this, too, brings him more scolding and more slaps with that noisy newspaper, he begins to see a great light. By a long or short process of elimination, according to his rating in intelligence tests, he is finally convinced that *none of the furniture* is for his use, but is strictly reserved for the human members of the family.

Yet you have neither broken his spirit nor shaken his confidence in either your affection or your good judgment. Why not? What's the difference between this case and that of your trousers or skirt? You have already sensed it. When he put on his jumping act he was, as we know, living up to his credo by trying to please *you.* When he chose the davenport for a siesta he did it to please *himself,* and he has brains enough to know it. He may think it strange you should object, but he's not particularly puzzled about it. After all, it's your furniture, not his, and you have a right to do as you please with your own.

I have dealt with this and the preceding case in what may seem unnecessary detail because they are illustrations of the two types into which dog faults naturally fall and which I promised to analyze. As for the cures, it's unnecessary to repeat that the newspaper and the sharp command "Down!" when used in the jump-up situation are wrong in principle, and that the newspaper and the sharp warning, "No, no!" used in the davenport case are right in principle. If you will keep these two examples in mind and apply them as a yardstick to each succeeding problem as it comes up, you will simplify things considerably.

Suppose you try it right now. How about that housebreaking business? Please stop reading at this point, put this book on the table and pause to think it over for class identification.

*   *   *   *   *

The stars indicate a lapse of three or four minutes and your thinking has probably led you to the following conclusion.

Since you recall the statement that dogs and even pups are naturally cleanly in their habits, your yardstick tells you that when Jock, neat in his own house, is careless and untidy in yours, he is acting, not in line with his natural instincts, but against them. This puts this misdemeanor definitely in Class Two and makes scolding and corporal punishment justifiable. Most of us have seen a pup that has never been so much as reproved for untidiness indoors appear so ashamed and sheepish after his first serious *faux pas* of the kind that he was positively funny.

CHAPTER X

"Sit" and "Down"

FOND of Jock as you are, there are times when he is very much in the way — not to say a nuisance. So are human youngsters now and again, even our own. So it's nothing to be excited about. But it *is* something to be taken in hand before it goes too far.

When you stand talking to an acquaintance you meet in the park or on the street, Jock should sit quietly at your side until the conversation — presumably a short one — is over and all three of you move on. During that much longer conversation with a friend under the elm on your lawn he should lie comfortably at your feet — *yours,* remember — and stay put until you give him permission to rise.

We'll first consider the case of you and the man or woman in the park or on the street because it comes first in point of time. Jock should be taught to sit before he learns to obey the command "Down!" for a reason I'll explain shortly. To attempt even the former before the pup is five or six months old is a mistake. Before that he "hasn't got what it takes" to sit quietly at your side or anywhere else unless he feels like it, and to force him to do it is not only unwise and difficult — it's cruel.

There are various more or less intricate mechanical methods for teaching a pup to sit and hold his position until further orders; and I have no doubt they are efficient. But unfortunately I'm no mechanic. What's more, if I ever brought myself to consider a puppy a piece of machinery, I should instantly lose all interest in him.

I have an idea you will find teaching your pupil to sit about the easiest of all your training work. The system, if you can call anything so simple a system, requires four things: your leash, your common sense, a little patience and that priceless tidbit in-your pocket.

Choose a time when you and Jock are alone and he has become a trifle tired from play or a long run and for that reason a short rest will very likely be in line with his own inclinations. Call him to you, slip the leash over his head, hold it loosely in your right hand and stand talking to him as he looks up at you to listen. Now say "Sit!" or the more popular "Hup!" just a bit sharply to distinguish it from your conversational tone. But if there is even a remote possibility you will ever want to train Jock for the official obedience tests that are now a feature of many dog shows, don't

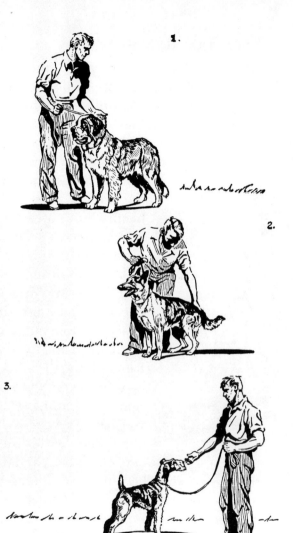

1.

2.

3.

TEACHING DOG TO SIT

1. Slip the Leash over His Head
2. Hold Leash and Press on Rump
3. Give Him Reward

say "Hup!" It is enough like "Hop!", the command to jump used in these tests, to be very confusing. If there is no such possibility I think you will find "Hup!" preferable — it has more kick to it.

As you say "Hup!" or "Sit!" as the case may be,

"HOLD IT!"

hold up Jock's head with the leash in your right hand, lean over and with your left hand press steadily on his rump until he is in a sitting position. If he flops over to one side, you can easily straighten him out with your left hand on his flank. Almost the instant he is in the proper position, slip him the tidbit you have in your right hand, release the pressure on his body and the

pull on the leash. When he jumps to his feet, as he almost certainly will, give him the order "All right!" or, better yet, simply cluck to him as your father or grandfather used to cluck to his old mare, Nellie. I like this clucking sound better than any articulate word because it can be used in a number of similar situations and because it can never be confused with any other command. This is especially important in this case and the others like it we shall discuss later, since it invariably gives an order your pup is willing and even anxious to obey. When that is true, you should not only stick religiously to one form of command; you should make it individual and distinctive. If you do not, your pup is likely to take almost anything you say as the order he is impatient to hear.

As soon as you have given Jock his reward, pat him on the head once or twice or give him a friendly slap on the shoulder, at the same time telling him he's a good dog. Now wait a few moments to allow the pup a little respite, then go through the same routine again. But never make the lesson too long. The moment Jock shows signs of being tired or losing interest, ring the bell for school's out.

With each successive lesson make the intervals between "Hup!" and the cluck longer and longer. Once the pup gets the idea firmly fixed in his mind, your progress and his will be reasonably rapid.

When he thoroughly understands what you want and obeys promptly and cheerfully, you and he can go ahead and polish things up. You now quit holding the leash in your hand; but let Jock keep on wearing it. You will find it has a certain restraining effect, and you can always pick it up when things don't click as they should.

Put Jock through this lesson at least once a day until he sits correctly and makes no move to rise until he hears your cluck. And since you now

"HUP!"

have both hands perfectly free, you can use your index finger held up as a warning gesture, to accompany and emphasize the word "Hup!" which you repeat whenever necessary.

To keep Jock in his place use the words "Hold it!", "Stay there!" or anything you please when and if he starts to get on his feet again. But use the same words each time and the same gesture with the index finger.

So far, so good. Your pup now obeys the command "Hup!" or "Sit!" and stays put until he hears that welcome cluck. But up to this point you have always stood directly in front of him — almost over him, in fact. Now he must learn to obey the three commands — to sit, to stay seated and to rise — when you are not directly in front of him and much farther away; even when you may be paying no attention to him whatever.

To accomplish this, begin by walking slowly backward as he sits in position. He will want to follow and will start to do so. Hold up that warning finger, repeat the commands "Hup!" and "Hold it!", go back to him slowly, take him by the collar and put him back exactly where he was, never forgetting to accompany the action with the command "Hup!" and, if Jock is the sort of pup to require it, add a light tap or two with the loose end of his leash. Give him no reward of merit at this point; simply cluck, wait a little while and go through the same maneuver again. Don't keep him waiting too long before *you go back to him* to cluck and give him his tidbit. Never, under any circumstances, give him the cluck signal until you have reached him, and don't even let him do any edging up to meet you. Let X mark the spot where you originally placed him and see that he stays there. This is imperative.

From this point on it is merely a matter of varying your movements to accustom Jock to all kinds of situations. For a starter you simply turn your back on him as you walk away instead of walking backwards to face him. Turn after a step or two, though, to catch him in time if he tries to "beat the barrier." That's a case where it's important to know exactly where he was originally sitting — why, as we said, some X you have selected — like a small stone or a bare place in the lawn —

should mark the spot. Later on you walk slowly behind him and back on the other side, and so forth.

A tough job, you think? Then let me tell you that when I was a small boy I taught my first puppy, Spot, to sit and watch a nice tasty bit of meat placed on the stable floor directly in front of him and so close he could grab and eat it without moving an inch. In a very short time I had him so thoroughly trained I used to invite a crowd of schoolmates for an audience, place little Spot and the meat in their proper position, leave the pup and the boys flat, and go upstairs to the stable loft. Then I would knock boxes around and make a general racket for five minutes, then come down to find Spot, the meat, and, as a rule, even the audience, just as I had left them. The boys were so fascinated by the exhibition they didn't move — just stood and gaped. After enjoying my triumph for a moment or two I clucked to Spot, the meat disappeared down his gullet in a flash and the curtain fell to thunderous applause. Yet I was no better trainer than you will be, probably not as good, for I was pretty young. And I had never read a book on training or received one word of oral instruction from anybody. That's how much of an expert you have to be.

Just a moment for our usual checkup. It's obvious to Jock your command is perfectly reasonable because you are only asking him to do for you what he very often does for himself — take a seat. To be sure, you ask him to hold his position longer than he might of his own accord, but, once he knows what you want and that it's nothing against his instinct or principles, he's glad to comply.

As in all other cases in which the tidbit is used, it is merely a temporary expedient, and you and Jock will soon forget it. Your words of praise and a pat or two on the head will be reward enough. That "aim to please" slogan of his is for use, not merely to hang on the wall, like "God Bless Our Home."

Which brings us more or less gracefully out under the big elm on the lawn and to the command "Down!" But, if I were you, I wouldn't be in too much of a dither about that as yet. One reason is that, with Jock already obedient to the command to sit, the additional training necessary to teach him to "down" is so simple it can be done at any time. The other reason concerns, not only your best interests, but the best interests of the pup himself. I like to flatter myself I have a certain understanding of dog and pup nature — that I am able to put myself in their places to a certain extent. I'm probably a mile off in this assumption, but if I'm one per cent right about it, it's a bad idea to do anything that tends to lessen the self-

confidence and spirit of young puppies. I like to
see them bold and upstanding — on their toes, as
we say. To learn to sit up, watchful and alert,
waiting for your next command, does not, I think,
destroy or even dampen their spirit. To force
them to lie prone at your feet in an attitude of
abject submission has a tendency, I think, to do
one or both of these things. For the average pup
of five months or less is only too apt to have a
ready-made inferiority complex of his own and
does enough getting down on his belly and crawling around like a worm when he's corrected or
even spoken to, without being *taught* to do it. But
by the time he's seven or eight months of age,
especially if he's been wisely handled and well
trained, he begins to feel his oats. He obeys the
commands he has learned because he's crazy about
you and respects you, but he has acquired or is
rapidly acquiring a whole lot of respect for himself, too. He considers himself a dog now — not a
puppy — and wants the world and his wife to consider him the same way. This, I think, is the time
when it will do no harm to take a little of the con-
ceit out of him — in your usual tactful way. And
right here let me stress the importance of keeping
Jock up to concert pitch in all the accomplishments he has acquired up to this point. See to it
there is no backsliding on his part. If there has

been, you have been a backslider too — with much less excuse.

Now for the order "Down!" and the correct response to it. I promised to show you the latter would be comparatively easy to get, and I think you already see why that is so. It's simply one step further in the "sit" routine Jock already knows so well, and in this case well begun is nine tenths done instead of only one half.

Give Jock the order to sit, then slip the leash over his head and stand facing him, holding the leash loosely in your left hand. Now stoop quickly, hold up your right hand, palm down, as a mild threat of a slap, pull sharply downward on the leash with your left hand to bring Jock down to a crouch and at the same moment say "Down!" sharply — and you make your tone good and sharp. If necessary, which is doubtful, you put your left hand on the pup's shoulder and force him down, as you forced his rear end when you taught him to sit. He may flop over and beg for mercy as he possibly did in his first "sit" lesson, but he's an older and bolder pup now, and the chances are he will take the proper pose or something approximating it. Whether he does or not, let it go for the present, cluck him up again, give him his tidbit, word of praise and pat on the head; and the job from then on is exactly the same as in the "sit" lessons. By which I mean you make the intervals between the "Down!", accompanied by the palm-down gesture, and the cluck longer and longer, teach him to stay put by repeating the "Down!" and gesture when necessary, and see to it he lies in his original place, no matter where you may go or what you may do. You do all this exactly as in the "sit" sessions.

As for his exact pose, that's a matter for you to decide. The chances are, as Jock becomes accustomed to the command and obedience to it, he will look on it more and more casually, and in time will make his posture fit any given situation as he sizes it up. When he makes up his mind you are all set for a long conversation with a friend, he will probably turn over on his side and take a nap.

In similar situations inside the house or at the home of a friend, Jock, if properly trained, will lie anywhere you say and stay there, completely out of the social picture, until you give him permission to join the company. This is simply another practical application of the training already described and requires no further explanation as to technique. But Jock's obedience to the order and gesture "Down!" will prove an especial blessing when you and he go calling. Dogs, as you have learned, are inquisitive to a degree and love to explore new territory. When Jock, through lack

TEACHING DOG TO "DOWN"

1. Give Order to Sit and Slip Leash over Head
2. Pull Downward on Leash and Say "Down!"
3. If Necessary, Force Him Down with Hand

of proper training, persists in nosing around through the rooms of a house in which you are a caller or visitor, it is not only embarrassing to you, but may be a cause of constant apprehension to your host or hostess.

If you happen to be interested, the strict letter of the law requires that a dog, at the command "Down!", should lie flat on his belly, his hind legs drawn forward and partly under him and his paws extended forward — the pose of the stone or bronze lions *couchant* with which sculptors are fond of adorning the entrances of libraries. You may, if you have the inclination, time and patience, or if you intend going in for the obedience-test game later on, insist on this. I suppose I should blush to admit it, but when a dog of mine lies quietly at my feet until I cluck to him to get up, he may take any old position he pleases, provided it isn't so immodest as to be embarrassing. Some men — and exceedingly clever and sensible ones — always click their heels sharply when bowing on being presented to a woman. Others — equally clever and sensible — never do. So there you are!

CHAPTER XI

Coming to Heel and Staying There

JOCK, as you are learning by the minute, is no longer a baby; he's nearly eight months old. Your daily walks with him have become more and more interesting as you and he have grown to know and understand each other better. He obeys your whistle or call promptly and cheerfully as a rule; but now and then, when temptation is strong, he pays little or no attention to either. In such cases, settle the matter then and there. But be fair to both yourself and your pup. Don't lose your head and yell at him angrily, *never, in any but the most critical situation, run toward him,* and even then not in a threatening way. He is smart enough to know he has four legs to your two and is a much more artful dodger.

Simply remain where you are, get down on your haunches, hold out your hand, palm up, in an enticing way, snap your fingers, repeat your whistle, and call to him as persuasively as you know how. Jock will subconsciously connect your outstretched hand with the tidbit he used to get; your crouching position brings you down to his level and indicates you have not lost your temper, and the tone of your voice is reassuring. You might even turn and trot a few steps *farther away* from the pup, then turn and repeat the

crouching act. The whole combination is one most pups find very hard to resist.

If Jock falls for it and comes to you, give him two or three pats and a rub or two behind his ears as you praise him for being obedient. If he still holds his ground he has committed a Class Two offense by deliberately disobeying a command he understands and knows is

TEACHING DOG
TO COME WHEN
CALLED

reasonable. So walk slowly toward him, still whistling or calling in a firm tone, take him by the collar and give him a few light cuts with your leash, not forgetting to whistle as you punish him. Slip the leash over his head, lead him back to the point where you were when you first whistled, and go on with your walk, keeping him on leash long enough to make him realize it is additional punishment.

Failure to handle this particular situation properly is one of the commonest mistakes made by amateur trainers. Don't put yourself in their class. *Never punish a dog when at your command he comes to you of his own free will,* even if it has required repeated calling, or even cajolery, to bring him. The dog can draw but one conclusion — that he is getting a whipping for coming at all. He'll try not to make the same blunder again. Punish him at the place where he disobeyed or not at all. Otherwise you are inflicting a penalty suited to a Class Two crime on a dog that has actually committed no crime whatever except that of being a little hesitant in obeying an order.

But Jock, though not a baby, is still a pup and has by no means outgrown puppy ways. Even when he comes to you promptly, there are times when you wish him to stay close to you until the strange dog, timid child, approaching motorcar, or whatever he may annoy or injure or that may annoy or injure him, is well out of the way. Sometimes this attraction is interesting or exciting enough to make Jock a bit hard to control. You then have an active and eager pup darting in and out between your legs, getting in your way every other step and possibly even tripping you up. The leash only adds to your troubles since it almost invariably becomes entangled in your legs or encircles them and brings you to an abrupt and undignified stop. Or you may find yourself vio-

lently pulled forward by a determined front run-
ner or dragged backward with equal violence, as
the case may be. The pulling power of even a
small puppy is surprising.

To avoid this comedy of errors, you should
resort to that tidbit (a bit of puppy biscuit, a
kernel of buttered popcorn or

just a little piece of cracker),
keeping it in the hand that
holds the leash. When Jock discovers it he will come forward
or backward to get it and, without realizing what he's doing.
trot along at your side on a
loose leash just as you want him
to do. After a minute or two
give him the morsel he has been
following with his nose or eyes.
As was the case when you
taught him to obey the whistle
and to sit and "down," the tidbit will soon be unnecessary.
Correct conduct on leash will

LEASH SHOULD
BE IN LEFT
HAND WITH
TIDBIT

have become a habit. By correct conduct I mean
walking quietly close to your side, always remaining on the same side — preferably your left — and
with his head where you want it, which will probably be with his shoulder blades about even with
your left leg, so that you can take him by the collar

or give him a friendly pat on the head when you wish.

One more detail. It is as important that Jock leave you properly when you take off his leash as it is that his manners be good when he's wearing it. To teach him this requirement, again choose a time and place when and where there is as little

"CORRECT CONDUCT" WHILE WALKING

as possible to distract his attention, stop walking, wait a few seconds, then quietly remove his leash and take a firm hold on his collar. Wait another moment or two until Jock is perfectly calm, then take your hand from his collar, at the same time saying "Go on, Jock!", "All right, Jock!" or use the cluck signal as you did after the commands "Hup!" and "Down!"

Whether you use a spoken order or the cluck, accompany it with an encouraging wave of the hand, if that is necessary; but the chances are you will find it is not.

These requirements for good manners when out for a walk are quite enough for you to teach or for Jock to learn before he is at least six or seven

TEACHING DOG TO LEAVE LEASH PROPERLY

months old. If he is a little backward, delay any further lessons even a month or two more. But the time has probably come when the use of your leash in cases like the one we have been discussing is an admission of lack of control on your part and a lack of education on the part of your nearly full-grown pup. This admission is anything but flattering to either of you. You know Jock should stay at your side without any mechanical compulsion until you give him permission to be off and away.

That is called "walking at heel," because years ago custom called for a dog that traveled directly behind his handler. This position is out of date today. For companionship's sake, easier control and to allow the dog to see ahead and so get more pleasure from his walk and quicker warning of possible danger, most modern owners prefer that he be at their left side, as already suggested. Then, too, most of us carry a bundle, package, suitcase, cane, gun, etc., etc., in our right hand. In many cases what we carry would be definitely in the way of a dog walking at our right, and the dog would definitely interfere with our carrying it. The left side is also better for the woman or young girl who appreciates the protection of an alert dog, since people she meets usually pass on her left.

The routine for teaching coming to heel can be guaranteed 100 per cent effective; yet the number of otherwise well-mannered dogs that have never been taught it or have been allowed to forget and disregard it is inexcusably large. This may be because the lessons, while simple enough in themselves, are none too readily learned as a rule and call for a good deal of patience on the part of the trainer; or because the accomplishment is not considered important.

Whatever the cause, the effect of this neglect to teach an essential is definite. One of the surest ways to gain a name for yourself as an expert trainer is to walk along a public street, your leash in your pocket and your dog walking dutifully at heel.

The reason why the lessons should be delayed until your pupil is fairly well grown you already understand. It's another case of a young pup being too irresponsible and harum-scarum to make real progress probable. And since walking quietly at heel in all sorts of surroundings and under all sorts of temptations requires much more self-control than either sitting at your side or lying at your feet, the instruction required to teach it should follow and not precede the other two.

Another determining factor is that lessons in coming to heel and staying there will require the use of a light whip or switch as well as a leash. This makes waiting until such time as the pup has acquired a certain amount of cockiness still more necessary than was the case with the other two accomplishments. The switch, however intelligently you use it, has a tendency to make even a bold pup a little apprehensive and a congenitally timid one permanently man-shy.

The actual training required is, in relation to training to handle well on leash, exactly like the relation between teaching lying and sitting. In each case the second is a natural corollary to the first. You are merely going to ask your pup to do on his own responsibility, and without physical restraint of any kind, precisely what he has already learned to do with a loose leash around his neck. The procedure is this:

When you take Jock for his usual walk and run, carry with you, in addition to your usual leash and tidbit, the light whip or switch we just mentioned. Choose a favorable time just as in the other lessons, stop, remove the leash, wait a moment or so, say "Heel!", then continue walking slowly *without clucking the "go" signal Jock may be expecting*. Knowing he is free, he will probably decide you have forgotten to give him the word and dash out ahead on his own responsibility.

Stay where you were, call him back to you, and put on his leash, say "Heel, heel!" firmly and walk a little way with Jock still wearing the leash. Stop after a few yards, remove the leash, stand still for a moment or two, then start forward again repeating "Heel!", but be ready to take the pup by the collar if he starts to leave his proper position. Don't be afraid to jerk him a bit as you repeat the order to heel. But the moment he begins to get the idea, don't keep him waiting for the cluck signal. Give it to him when you have taken two or three steps ahead and he is still at your side, gradually increasing the time as he begins to understand what is expected of him. And make the lessons short. Even when they go smoothly they are something of a strain on both you and your pupil.

For some time after Jock has learned what you want him to do and does it after a fashion, you will find him working his way too far forward, trying to switch over to your right side instead of staying at your left or occasionally lagging behind. As a preventive carry the switch in your right hand and in your left your leash and that old reliable tidbit. As you walk swing the leash with a circular motion at right angles to your body in such a way that Jock will get it on the nose if he pushes too far ahead on your left. If he changes to your right tap his nose lightly with the switch. When he lags behind speak to him and bring him up to the proper position — with the aid of the tidbit if necessary. In every case be sure to repeat the command "Heel, heel!"

That's all there is to it, but as I've said, it will win you a reputation. When I was a very small boy in the country, a man by the name of Cass used to pass Father's place every day or so during the hunting season, a gun on his shoulder, his pipe in his mouth and two rather nondescript little setters walking like a well-matched team of draft horses, side by side, directly behind him. When he stopped to talk to someone he met or to light his pipe, the dogs stopped too, and stood quietly,

TEACHING DOG TO HEEL

1. *Remove Leash*
2. *Restore Leash and Walk a Little Way*
3. *Swing Leash to Keep Dog from Pushing too Far Ahead on Left*

never changing their relative positions. When their master went on again, they followed as before.

I didn't know then and don't know now whether Cass was a good man with a dog in any other respect; but I shall never forget my admiration for him as a trainer. I felt that teaching *one* dog to walk at heel was a job for an expert. The man who could teach *two* to do it together and to do it so perfectly must be, I thought, nothing less than a genius. Yet all the man needed to perform what I considered a miracle was a pair of fairly intelligent dogs, a knowledge of any good training routine to fit the case and patience enough to apply it. And the greatest of these was patience.

CHAPTER XII

When Dog Meets Dog

Dogs are among the most socially inclined of all animals. They love company, whether it be that of humans, other animals or other dogs. The mutual affection that often exists between a horse and a dog is proverbial. Many a temperamental thoroughbred is encouraged to do his best on the track by the inspiring barks of the devoted little pal that shares his stall. Dogs and cats are, in theory, natural enemies, but when they live together in the same household almost invariably become fast friends. A female dog mothering and even nursing orphaned kittens is such a common occurrence it hardly rates a news item in the local paper. It would be difficult to find a four-footed animal or even any species of bird that the average dog will not accept as a friend and companion if conditions are favorable.

Since this is true, it is no wonder Jock takes delight in meeting others of his kind, and that when such meetings occur you usually find everything is lovely and the tails wag high. The introduction may take place in your home when a friend and his dog drop in for a call, or outside, when you and Jock are taking a walk and both dog and owner are strangers. In either case your interference is not only unnecessary but inconsiderate. In the park or on the street the little formalities all dogs seem to think constitute good form are quickly over as a rule and the two go their respective ways, each rejoicing in the fact that he has made another acquaintance.

There will be times, however, when the pair are so congenial they immediately want to run and romp together. Unless you, or the other owner, are in a hurry it's a good idea to let them have their fun for a few minutes, since both will be benefited by the more or less violent exercise they might not get in any other way. But you will make sure Jock is always under control by whistling him in now and then, tactfully choosing a moment when he can obey without too violent conflict between his sense of duty on the one hand and his inclinations on the other. Be sure, too, you anticipate Jock's sudden rush to greet the other dog by a warning "Heel!" followed almost immediately by "All right, Jock!", cluck or whatever your "go" signal may be. You should be tactful, too, in selecting an opportune moment to decide enough is enough, call your dog to heel and go on with your walk.

Unfortunately the agreeable social amenities we

have described as usual when two dogs meet do not invariably take place as advertised. Sometimes it's a case of Greek meeting Greek. If both belligerents are on leash, it may be a tug of war; but even if neither is properly trained the owners have the situation well in hand. If either dog is free and under poor control, a battle may be imminent. This calls for prompt but *never excited* action.

Assuming that Jock is not the aggressor and his training to stay at heel has been thorough, the affair should be comparatively easy to handle, since you can confine your attention to the other dog, making him keep his distance or beat a retreat. But if, by any chance, you have your dog on leash, don't take advantage of the fact by pulling him forcibly away from his attacker. Dogs are extremely proud of their courage, and inclined to bluff even when they are scared stiff. Holding Jock back reflects on his willingness to fight and gives the psychological edge to his opponent. But you can forget this angle if Jock is a little fellow and a member of the toy group. In that case you simply pick him up in your arms and hold him out of harm's way. This will hurt neither his feelings nor his pride. On the contrary he will be pretty sure to take advantage of his temporary social security to be bold as a lion, bark his defiance at the other dog and do his best to indicate that, if he could only get down and at him, he would chew him to ribbons.

If Jock is a large or a medium-sized dog or a terrier the suggestions we have made should cover most cases where the strange dog is unaccompanied by his owner. When the latter is on the spot to lend a hand the situation is, of course, doubly simple.

No matter what precautions you may take, fights, like accidents, are sometimes bound to happen. When they do, you will discover that different breeds and even different individual dogs have differing systems of attack and defense. Collies, for example, commonly rush in, snap viciously, retreat, rush in again and repeat the snap. English bull terriers spar for an opening just as human wrestlers do, and when they see it go in like a flash, get a grip on a vulnerable spot, like the throat, and hang on like snapping turtles.

What to do about it? If the battlers are at your home or that of a friend, use the water cure, or, in desperate situations, the ammonia mixture prescribed for incorrigible barkers and automobile chasers. (This is discussed in Chapter XV.) For here's a case where it will do no harm. Both dogs are too excited and angry to know what is done to stop them or to care who does it.

On the street or anywhere else where no water is available, adapt your tactics to those of the fighting dogs. If either is using the snap-and-get-away system, grab him by the collar as he jumps back for a plunge, keeping the other fighter away by shouts, kicks or any way you cán. But keep cool and don't lose your head, and never kick or strike the dogs when they are at actual grips. It only adds fuel to the fire. This is equally true of grabbing either or both contestants by the tail or hind leg and trying to pull the pair apart. And it's bad business to step in between them. You may be badly bitten if you try it.

Whatever style of fighting the scrappers may choose you can often use your slip-over leash to shut off the wind of your dog while the owner of the other chokes his. A leash is preferable to the bare hand because there is less *likelihood* of being bitten; it is also less tiring and even more effective for choking purposes. Its only disadvantage is that it is sometimes difficult or awkward to get it into place. If it can be used on only one of the dogs pick the one that has the death grip. Naturally you can't slip the leash over his head, but by running the hand loop end through the slip noose, you get the same result. If both owners are on the job and both adopt the garroting system, the fight will soon be over. But look out for ructions the next time the two dogs meet. The contest was a draw as far as they were concerned and each will be spoiling for a return battle.

As already said, most dogs are friendly. They are also good sports as a rule and almost never bother a much smaller dog that knows he hasn't a chance and admits it by rolling over on his back and crying quits before the fight can even get going. But don't ever expect any one of the terriers to beg for mercy, no matter how small he may be. If he's a member of the lodge in good standing he'll tackle an Irish wolfhound or pit bull with a cheerful disregard for consequences that is a credit to his courage but a slam at his common sense.

As for Jock, if he's a good-sized dog and happens to be the kind that goes around with a chip on his shoulder, it will do him no harm to take a thorough trouncing from a better dog than he is; and if you are wise you will allow him to get it. If that doesn't teach him a lesson and he keeps on throwing out his chest and growling a challenge to every strange dog he meets, there's nothing much to do but slap him down with your leash and slap him down hard. You need have no fear of breaking his spirit or making him man-shy. You could break his head first. If he still persists in looking for trouble — and I've known a few dogs that would — there's nothing much you can do except to hope you get a rabid pacifist as his successor when he passes on. It's safe to say that, taking him brawl for brawl, you will not care to own his like again.

CHAPTER XIII

Good Motor Manners,
Inside and Outside the Car

You probably still recall that hectic motor trip — the one that introduced you to Jock and his jittery stomach and seemed interminable. Let's hope it is now only an amusing memory. If Jock is like most pups, any uneasiness you may feel about the pup-automobile combination arises from the fact that he has made a complete right-about-face and has a perfect mania for motoring. That is a great satisfaction in many ways, but in others it may be serious. Certain dogs will jump into the open door of any car they find standing anywhere, whether occupied or not, a weakness well known to dog thieves. Or Jock may have enough self-control or be sufficiently exclusive to confine his riding to your own car or cars, and still be a source of both annoyance and worry. His lack of good manners may be embarrassing and he may do things that make riding dangerous to you both as well as to any other passengers in the car.

He should be taught never to enter an automobile unless expressly ordered to do so by any command you may choose, such as "In, Jock!" or the cluck we have found so useful for two other orders. Here again the cluck gives permission to do something your pup is very anxious to do and he cannot pretend to confuse it with any other command and get away with it. You will notice I've suggested the use of "In, Jock!" instead of plain "In!" for this case. This is neither by chance nor by accident, but because it is an added protection against thieves who do not know the pup's name. So it's a good idea to precede the cluck, if you adopt it, with the name too. My reason for reversing the order if you use the cluck is that the latter has become a definite "go" signal to Jock and he'll wait for no additional hint. "In," on the contrary, is used in no other connection. Whatever form your command may take, hold the pup to it to prevent a free-for-all between the two of you to see who will be inside first.

Training for correct conduct in a car is exceedingly simple, although, as in the whole training proposition, you can't hurry it. The groundwork is vitally important; take plenty of time to get the fundamentals well fixed and the frills will be easy.

When Jock tries to scramble into your car without permission, which he undoubtedly will do every time he thinks he sees a ride ahead, jerk him back on his haunches sharply with your leash and give him the command to sit. See that he holds this position until you are in the car and seated at the wheel. Or, if you teach him his motoring manners *before* you teach him to sit, jerk him back in the same way, put yourself between him and the car, stand facing him and get into the car backwards. Still facing him so that you can flick his nose with the leash, repeat "No, no!" as often as necessary to keep him in his place and use your raised hand or index finger to make the order more emphatic. Now slide easily back of the wheel and sit in driving position. This whole series of moves should be very deliberate with plenty of time between each; and when you are at the wheel sit there for a moment or two before you say "In, Jock!" or cluck.

If by any chance Jock is timid or backward about climbing into the car, get in yourself as before, then use your leash or (if you are dealing with a very small pup) a cord considerably longer than the leash, as a persuader. Encourage the pup by your voice and whistle and, if necessary, sit on the running board and help him up to that point with a lift. But be sure you are always ahead of him with every new position you take, never behind him. In this, as in the other case, insist on obedience to your command or cluck. However retiring or even reluctant Jock may be at the moment, you'll find it absolutely necessary later, if you are to escape that free-for-all to see who is in first.

Once you are both inside the car, opinions differ as to what is cricket and what is not. Some say dogs should never ride on the front seat, since they may interfere with the driver at some critical moment. That sounds sensible, but suppose your car is a coupé and Jock must ride on the seat with you or not at all. It's best, I think, to let him sit beside you if possible. It not only looks rather smart but it keeps him where you can see him at all times without actually turning your head. He can also see better and get better air; but don't allow the wind to blow too strongly in his face. It is injurious to both his eyes and his ears, and a dog's ears are extremely susceptible to canker. Keep your windshield closed if you would escape a veterinary bill or the expenditure of a deal of time and trouble in treating Jock for either canker or sore eyes.

Sore eyes are, of course, perfectly evident to anyone at a glance. Canker is a little more elusive. If for no obvious reason Jock shakes his head rapidly from side to side as he sits or stands, examine his inner ear for inflammation or have a veterinary do it for you.

If you don't care to have Jock sit erect, he should lie quietly beside you so that he will in no way interfere with your vision or in any other way make driving dangerous. Never, under any circumstances, allow your dog to ride on your running board or hood unless you are "taking him for a ride" in the underworld meaning of the phrase.

Whatever location you select as Jock's *regular* riding place, don't let him get the idea he *cannot ride in any other part of the car* when ordered to do so. There are bound to be times when his customary position at your side on the front seat will be exceedingly inconvenient for you or someone riding with you. Or you may have Jock with you when riding in a friend's car and the pup's persistence in trying to monopolize a spot on the front seat will be a nuisance to you and everybody else concerned. So, during the lessons described in the following paragraphs, vary the routine *after the fundamentals are thoroughly taught*. Have Jock ride on the rear seat for fifteen minutes or longer now and then, or lie on the floor in front of it or even on the floor under the cowl.

To teach any desired posture and location, your early instructions should be given when the car is stationary and you can therefore devote your entire attention to your pupil. Whistle and call him up on the seat beside you, if necessary, which will very seldom be the case. Give him the command to sit or lie. If he has not learned the meanings of these two orders, now is an excellent time to teach him the preliminaries, directions for which you have already read. The situation is especially favorable due to the fact that you are practically down to his level for the whole series of training requirements and, as an added advantage, Jock cannot get away from you and probably will not want to.

When he understands the order to sit or lie, obeys promptly and holds his position until you give him the cluck signal, *then and not until then, start your engine but not your car*. It may be a number of days before he learns this routine, but don't be impatient. Take your time and plenty of it.

If Jock stays put when the motor starts to hum, wait a minute or two before getting under way. Speak to him casually in a quiet voice, give him a friendly pat or two, and start slowly and smoothly forward. If he shows signs of excitement at the prospect of a ride, stop the car, keep the engine running and go through your training routine again. Only when he sits or lies quietly when you are moving very slowly should you make any attempt to reach even subnormal road speed.

To be on the safe side, when you actually put the car in motion choose, if possible, a place where there is little or no prospect of meeting another car, or of having another car pass you at high speed. Personally I have always used a short leash at this point, the noose end slipped over the gear-shift lever or hand brakes. This practice has been pretty generally condemned and with good reason. But if you make sure the strap is short enough to prevent the possibility of Jock getting any part of his anatomy, even a front or hind leg, outside your roadster or other open car, it helps. If the leash is six or eight inches too long, you may find yourself chief mourner at a dog funeral.

Once more, don't expect too much too quickly. If, after a week or two, Jock waits with obvious impatience and many protesting whines until you are at the wheel before scrambling in beside you, he deserves a medal. If he waits patiently and uncomplainingly, he will probably die young. He's too angelic for this world.

The above seems to cover correct conduct in your car fairly well, but what about the pup-automobile proposition when Jock is *not* in your car? What if he is chasing someone else's car in a desperate attempt to catch it, barking hysterically as he runs, entirely oblivious of the fact that he may finish as a hit-and-run victim of any one of the scores of reckless drivers who like to burn up the road? Jock's mad dashes usually occur when he has free run of your front yard and has sold himself the idea that chasing passing cars is not only perfectly legitimate but a wonderfully fascinating outdoor sport.

Since dogs, like people, are none too willing to give up a favorite game, curing a confirmed auto chaser may prove a difficult job. So try to convince Jock the sport isn't what he thought it was before it becomes a real hobby. By this time you should have no trouble keeping him in to heel, so we'll confine ourselves to the occasions when he's out in

AN EFFECTIVE WAY TO BREAK
DOG OF CAR CHASING

the yard on his own recognizance, as the lawyers put it.

The safest, most humane and at the same time most effective preventive for all ordinary cases is a piece of broom handle, or, with very small dogs, a similar stick of less diameter cut to the required length. Notch the stick in the middle and at that point tie a strong cord, so that when you tie the other end of the cord to Jock's collar the stick will hang as nearly horizontal as possible and be at the right point to hit his front legs when he runs.

For a medium-sized dog make the stick a foot or eighteen inches long and work up or down from that figure according to the size of your pup. Be sure it's long enough to be very awkward and annoying and likely to trip him. After being thrown end over end a few times he will probably be a sorer and wiser pup and discover that auto chasing as a sport is beginning to lose its appeal.

A second method requires the services of two confederates, both strangers to Jock, and an open car that is equally unfamiliar to him. Operator Number One drives the car; Number Two conceals himself in the tonneau or crouches on the floor of the car just inside the right front door. The stage is now set and the performance can begin, the only "prop" necessary being a large bucket of cold water to be used by Operator Number Two.

The car is driven rapidly by your place as you watch from your window to view the proceedings, unseen by your pup. When Jock makes his customary dash for the street and shifts into high to catch up with the car, the driver regulates his speed to that of the pup so that the latter can range alongside and try to take a nip at the whirling wheels. When the pup and front wheels are in the right relative positions, Operator Number Two jumps up and douses the pup with a well-directed bucketful of cold water — a variation of the time-tried "water cure" used in reformatories for handling human incorrigibles. Twice out of three times a few drenchings of this kind will prove similarly effective with Jock.

A modification of this system is to substitute for the bucket or pail of water a knapsack sprayer with hose and nozzle attached. This should assure absolute accuracy of aim and make it possible to use a steady stream for a minute or two if the pursuing pup is persistent enough. I'll admit I have never seen this tried; I'm simply submitting it as a plausible suggestion.

In extremely obstinate cases I have known of a fifty-fifty solution of ammonia and water being used as a substitute for aqua pura alone. That's my idea of a desperate remedy and I'm not advising it, no matter how desperate the disease. It may cause man-shyness, which is far more serious than auto chasing and infinitely more difficult to cure. I've never resorted to ammonia and never shall.

One thing is sure; if you administer the ammonia treatment, and it fails to cure your dog, you have but one course left. You simply wait for some careless or exasperated motorist to put an end to the chaser's existence.

CHAPTER XIV

Time Out! Ten Minutes for Observation

MOST of us, I've discovered, like to talk about our own individual dogs and the clever, amusing and sometimes apparently dumb things they do. So you may not object to taking a few minutes from your training sessions with Jock for another little powwow about Jock himself.

You have already tabbed a number of interesting things in his mental and moral make-up — qualities that make a dog a dog — and have turned them to your own advantage. But unless you are exceptionally observing you may have overlooked certain *physical* characteristics of his that to you, as his teacher, will prove almost as interesting and nearly as useful in his schooling.

If you keep your eyes open you will at once notice three very pertinent facts: that Jock's sense of smell is infinitely more acute than yours; his hearing considerably better, and his eyesight better in some ways and much poorer in others — in other words, entirely different. As for taste and touch, you and he differ but little in either, and

since that difference counts not at all in your training, we'll forget it and take up the three senses
that will be of practical value.

Few of us, I think, give much thought to the
marvelous piece of mechanism that is a dog's nose.
Let's compare it with a man-made device that has
nothing to do with the sense of smell, but is a fair
sample of scientific accuracy as applied to modern
mechanics.

I've read that at one of the big steel plants they
impress important visitors by drilling a small hole
in a one-ton block of steel and tooling a little bar of
the same metal to fit it. Both processes are done
with such accuracy that, while the bar easily slips
in and out of the hole, when it is inserted the
naked eye cannot detect where the block ends and
the bar begins. Then comes the dramatic moment.
The bar is removed from the block, the tempera-
ture of the block raised ten degrees, *and the bar
will no longer enter the hole.* The infinitesimal ex-
pansion of the block prevents it. Mechanical accuracy plus.

Now what has the nose of an ordinary everyday
hound to offer in the accuracy line? At one o'clock
some frosty fall morning a fox trots along a brushy
hillside hoping to pick up an unsuspecting rabbit.
Five hours later a hound strikes his trail. What
happens? If scenting conditions are poor the dog
may follow the trail in the wrong direction for a

hundred yards or even more before he decides he's backtracking and goes into reverse. If scenting conditions are good it will require only a hundred feet, or in some cases only fifteen or twenty, to get him going right. But we'll call it a hundred.

The fox covered that distance in about ten seconds. Which means the hound's nose was so incredibly sensitive it detected *a difference of ten seconds in age* between two sets of footprints *made five hours before.* Compared to that brand of black magic the steel block and bar were as crude as a ten-cent tape measure.

Granting that a foxhound is a scenting specialist, and that Jock may be anything from a great Dane to a Chihuahua, you will still find the latter's nose sufficiently sensitive to be useful to you as well as to him; and you should make the most of it. You did so, you remember, during his housebreaking lessons and by the use of that tidbit when you taught him to walk properly at heel. From now on you will discover it is not only increasingly valuable in your training operations, but interesting and instructive too.

You will be amused, for instance, to see how much more confidence he has in his nostrils than in his eyes or ears. When you come home from the office or a trip to town, your voice, general appearance and characteristic movements make him believe you are the man or woman he's been waiting for — his master or mistress. But he rarely fails to sniff at your hand or clothing to be sure of it. Dogs with normal noses are seldom fooled by a mirror. Jock's eyes may tell him there's another dog looking at him through a wooden frame, but his nostrils say "No." That's the pay-off and he doesn't bother to take a second look. They say a dog talks at both ends — with his tongue and with his tail. It is equally true that he has two sets of brains — one between his ears and the other at the end of his nose. When Jock has graduated from preparatory school and his higher education begins, the set at the end of his nose will be invaluable, as we shall see. Without it, he would be practically worthless as a watchdog, the number and variety of tricks you may wish to teach him would be limited to almost none, the most interesting requirements for obedience tests could never be met, and, in a word, a majority of the refinements and accomplishments that should make Jock an individual personality, not just a dog, could never be taught.

Yet there are times when Jock's supersensitive nose may be annoying. For a dog's taste in odors is very different from yours or mine. It doesn't make sense that an animal with such delicate olfactory nerves should be able to endure, much less enjoy, some of the awful smells he seems to consider a rare treat. Conversely, the subtle fragrance

of your expensive French perfumery will probably make him dig his nose into the dirt and
rub it with his paws to be rid of what, to him,
is an irritating or even disgusting scent.

All we need say about Jock's hearing is that he
can catch any sound you can and many you cannot,
like that soundless whistle, for instance. When it
comes to distinguishing one sound from another almost identical, he has you beaten by the proverbial
city block. The dog that instantly distinguishes the
sound of his master's car from that of all others,
even though they are of the same make and vintage,
is an example; and I've seen a litter of three-
months-old pups, every one of which was just as
clever.

The practical applications are many. Don't be
too ready to forgive Jock's disobedience on the
ground that he doesn't hear your command. Don't
lose your temper and let fly with a volley of verbal
abuse because you think he's too far away to hear
it. Nine times out of ten he does *hear* it and is
either too frightened or too cagey to let on. Dogs
are barefaced bluffers when they want to be.

Jock not only hears and identifies sounds surprisingly well; he connects them with the objects
or acts that usually accompany them. You already
know he does this in the case of spoken or whistled
commands, but you will find him capable of it
when you have given no command and don't even

suspect he is doing it. Remember this when some puzzling problem comes up, and consider whether hearing is a factor.

Last fall a gunner friend of mine was training his bird-dog pup. The youngster was always eager to hunt, but one morning he failed to show the slightest interest, simply tagging along at his master's heels. The man was mystified. Prince was in his usual perfect health, had no thorn in his foot, had not been punished or even scolded and had never shown himself a quitter. Conditions were in every respect exactly as they had been two days before, when the pup had been a regular dynamo in the brush.

Wait a minute. Were they, though? During the last two nights heavy frost had sent the leaves to the ground in showers. My friend thought a minute or two, smiled, took from his pocket a little brass bell, and attached it to Prince's collar. The mystery was solved. At the first tinkle the pup was himself again. The early season foliage had been heavy and Prince had never been hunted without a bell. He considered it a necessary part of his hunting kit and saw no sense in going to work without it.

To turn to the subject of eyesight, Jock's ability to see moving objects is superior to yours. With motionless objects it's just the opposite. Choose a time when he is busy burying a bone in your newly seeded lawn, step out onto the front porch and stand perfectly silent and motionless until he looks up and discovers you. Unless he catches your scent he probably registers mild curiosity or a trace of uneasiness perhaps, then goes on burying his bone. It's obvious he not only doesn't recognize you; he isn't even sure you are a human being. But make a move, however slight, and he's all attention in an instant, and your first familiar gesture or one word spoken in your natural voice brings him bounding to your side.

This looks like a case for an eye specialist; but here's another side to the picture. Two bird dogs, a setter and a pointer, competing against each other in field trials, race at top speed through ragweed or sedge, the judges and the handlers of the two dogs following on horseback a full quarter mile behind. Suddenly the handler of the setter stands in his stirrups, blows his whistle sharply and waves his wide-brimmed sombrero with a big sweep to his left. The setter hears the whistle above the rustle of the sedge, recognizes it as that of his handler, leaps into the air, head up, to catch the signal given with the hat, and swings to the left. The pointer goes on about his business, paying no attention whatever to the whistle, *because he knows it's not the one his handler uses*. Yet to you or me the two whistles sound precisely the same.

But aside from that angle, the setter, whose

vision for motionless things is no better than any other dog's, catches in a split second a signal given by one of a group of four or more horsemen over four hundred yards away, and so accurately that he distinguishes a wave to the left from a wave to the right without so much as a second glance. Apparently he doesn't need an oculist after all.

You realize, I'm sure, that the handler of the setter used a *combination* of two senses in getting obedience to his orders, just as you did when you taught Jock to sit or lie down by using both your voice and your upraised hand. If he could have utilized the sense of smell, as well as hearing and sight, he would have been that much better off. There will be times — when you begin training for obedience tests or trick work for instance — when you will be able to do that and, if you make the most of your opportunities, the results will occasionally be almost startling. In such exhibitions a well-trained performer will take directions from such slight clues as the flick of your finger, the surreptitious wink of your eye, a key word in a long sentence or the scent of an object he is asked to distinguish from a number that look identical.

Without going into further detail for the time being, our talk has brought to our attention the keenness of Jock's scenting powers, the acuteness of his hearing and his really remarkable ability to distinguish, one from another, two or more sounds that to us seem exactly alike. Also the peculiar quality of his eyesight that makes him notice a tiny brown wood mouse dodging into its hole under a tree, yet fail to recognize his own master standing quietly on the porch not twenty-five feet away. The more you study these phenomena — for they *are* phenomena — the better your equipment for making them play into your hands during your training of Jock. Even if this study had no bearing whatever on training, it is in itself a fascinating and highly instructive diversion.

CHAPTER XV

When Jock Talks Too Much

LIKE practically all dog owners, you are by this time pretty thoroughly prejudiced in favor of your own dog, Jock. You know he's well-bred because you have his pedigree to prove it; but you may sometimes forget that a dog can be both well-bred and ill-bred too. Ancestry and personal appearance to the contrary, socially he may be a boor. The acid test is his general reputation in the community in which you live. Like a spoiled child, he may be considered a perfect angel at home and a perfect pest everywhere else.

What's more to the point, the spoiled child frequently grows up to realize the mistakes his or her parents have made and correct them. You'll never see a dog with that much sense. Conversely, the most conscientiously and sensibly reared boy or girl may turn out a roughneck or a tomboy. A properly trained dog, handled with ordinary good judgment, never forgets to remember the lessons he learned when a pup. That's why to omit those lessons is indefensible.

Occupying a prominent place in the public-pest

class is the dog that dashes ahead of you to the door, barking like mad, when you admit a caller. This is a Class One fault — almost a virtue in fact — since it results from a praiseworthy wish to protect you; and for that reason the case should be handled with gloves.

If Jock begins barking the moment the bell rings or he hears the sound of the knocker, don't hurry to the door. Take time to silence him with the usual firm "No, no!" He has already learned what that command means and your quiet manner, together with your leisurely walk toward the door, implies there is nothing to be excited about. If he persists in barking as you walk, stop and repeat the order until he obeys before you go on again. Before you open the door give him another final warning, and make it fairly sharp if necessary. But unless Jock is a good bold dog and, in spite of his noisy greeting, inclined to be friendly with strangers, don't actually punish him for barking when he hears the bell or knocker. The remedy may well be worse than the disease. It's unnecessary to tell you it may lead to that man-shy complex, the biggest bluebottle in the whole training ointment. Besides, we have already filed this particular type of barking in the envelope marked Class One; so that sort of discipline is wrong in principle. You should be resourceful enough to cure the case correctly.

Much more annoying and difficult to reform is the confirmed and continuous barker or howler that vocalizes as a blanket protest against practically everything he sees and hears or merely for the pleasure he gets out of the noise he makes — definitely a Class Two proposition.

To own a barker of this type is not only a nuisance to you and your neighbors; in many cities and towns it is a misdemeanor. You must either cure your dog or get rid of him. Legal complications aside, most of us like to be on good terms with the family next door, yet few of us are keen about giving up a dog we have paid good money for, have become attached to, have gone to considerable trouble to train, and that has no really serious fault except that, like some of the rest of us, he talks too much.

If Jock is like the average pup, that concerto he performed during nearly the entire first night he spent at your home was, as we predicted, his farewell appearance on any stage. The sooner you convince him that from a pup's-eye view the world is a pretty good place to live in, the better for you and the neighborhood. The chances are this will be comparatively easy, especially if you pave the way with a preliminary or two.

One such preliminary is to serve him his final meal of the day as late in the evening as you conveniently can. A full stomach induces sleep, and although dogs, like people, sometimes talk in their sleep, the noises they make at such times wouldn't disturb a sufferer from chronic insomnia. A second anchor to windward is that piece of old carpet or sacking that you tacked over the door of his kennel. Be sure it is dropped down to close the opening fairly well. It will also keep Jock from "seein' things at night," which frequently aggravates if it doesn't actually cause the barking habit.

As for the cure itself, try the simple and obvious first. When Jock tunes up, stay in the house, but from your bedroom window call "No, no!" in your severest tones. It is very doubtful if this will do the trick, but try it just the same. Assuming this is a waste of breath, repeat the warning in the same severe tone and with a stick rap vigorously on anything that will make a good sharp noise, like a wooden table or your window sill. This may work and it may not. It is sure to prove a dud if you adopt the technique of a friend of mine who, at my suggestion, tried it out on her first pup.

The raps on the window sill were signally successful in attracting the attention of the pup, but from then on the system went haywire in a big way. It was not only a flat failure as a cure but turned out to be a positive bark producer in the bargain.

The way this woman operated was strictly as

per directions — with one perfectly excusable exception. Greatly embarrassed when her pet annoyed the neighbors at night, and not wishing to divert their attention from her dog to herself, her raps were anything but emphatic and she called "No, no!" in a soft crooning contralto that was sweet music to Yowler's ears. As we have already learned, dogs take their cue as much from the tone of our voices as from the words we speak, so the pup thought he was getting sympathy, not a scolding. Apparently he reasoned it out about as follows.

"I like to see my mistress and hear her talk kindly to me. When I bark or howl at night she comes to her window, hits the sill with a stick and calls 'No, no!' During the daytime 'No, no!' means 'Stop it!' and the stick is a warning I'd better watch my step; but at night it's entirely different. My mistress calls to let me know I'm not forgotten or maybe because she likes to have me bark after dark. It's either one or the other because she always speaks softly and tenderly to tell me I'm a good dog. As for the stick, she probably thinks that's a good way to attract my attention. I'm sure of one thing anyhow: when I'm lonesome at night and want the best company in the world, all I have to do is holler for it."

Following this faultless line of logic to its natural conclusion, this particular dog began barking whenever he felt lonesome during the daytime, which he had almost never done before taking the "cure."

Ingenious owners sometimes rig up a variation of the rap system in the form of a movable stick fastened to the outside of the kennel and operated from the owner's bedroom by a long wire or cord. When the concert at the kennel begins the owner swears softly and pulls the wire or cord violently with a series of quick jerks. The stick on the kennel raps its warning and the close proximity of the sound may impress the singer much or little, the amount depending on his credulity and desire to please.

A man in Pennsylvania has invented, tested and put in operation an elaborate variation of this method. He cures persistent nocturnal barkers by electrical transcription. The main features of his system consist of a push button in his bedroom, an insulated wire tapped into the ground side of the house wiring system and running from push button to kennel, a seven-watt light bulb which acts as a fuse, a wire running along the kennel chain and around the dog's collar, and various other (to me) mystifying gadgets. When the dog starts vocalizing the gifted gentleman in the bedroom presses the push button and gives the dog a shock.

One of the best cures is the use of a muzzle

of the common strap variety. Put it on your dog when he barks, and scold him as you adjust the straps, which you do in such a way that he can drink and pant comfortably, yet cannot open his mouth wide enough to produce a respectable bark or howl. This is a lifesaver in emergencies because *it is invariably successful temporarily,* even if it does not result in a permanent cure. For instantaneous results some night when the neighbors have reached the threatening stage, it is unsurpassed.

Already I hear you saying it's a cruel cure. But there's nothing cruel about an open strap muzzle properly put on; and it may prove a permanent cure for the barking habit.

Which brings us to the Class Two barker who makes a nuisance of himself during the daytime as well as at night. This annoyance is really a blessing in disguise. It's much more convenient to handle the case when you are up and about; and since the methods applicable for daytime use are to all intents and purposes exactly the same as those suggested for use after dark, they naturally tend to make the latter much more effective or even wholly unnecessary.

The muzzle system, for instance, is especially adapted to daytime training because the muzzle can be put on and taken off again as often as occasion requires. This *frequent repetition* of the punishment, accompanied each time by the scolding

necessary to make the pup understand it *is* a punishment, brings results, if at all, in a surprisingly
short time.

It's the same with the stick method. During the
day *you can go out to his kennel,* give Jock his
scolding, rap warningly on the side of the kennel with the stick, and if necessary punish him a
little with a folded newspaper or your leash.

In both these cases you have two definite advantages: you are dealing with your pup at close quarters, and you can inflict physical punishment if
it is needed.

As for the big bad wolf that resists all these comparatively mild correctives, he probably needs a
dose of the third degree — the water cure suggested in the last chapter for confirmed automobile
chasers. With this modification: you probably use
your lawn hose instead of the pail or bucket. If
you do, have the pressure on full and keep the
stream on the pup's head and face as continuously
as you can. To repeat to the point of boredom,
catch the culprit in the act and don't omit the
scolding.

If all else fails and you have reached a point
where you are resigned to ruining your dog if
the remedy doesn't work, substitute the knapsack
spray or a small garden sprayer for the lawn hose
and use that fifty-fifty solution of water and ammonia. But if you try it and get a cringing, crawl-

ing, man-shy neurotic for your pains, don't say it's my fault. I'm warning you now that the use of ammonia in this case is much more dangerous than in that of the motor maniac, for the good and sufficient reason that *the pup's master or mistress,* the man or woman he loves and trusts above all others, is the one who "does him wrong." Once a dog loses confidence in his best friend it's all over for both. I cannot size up your dog — you *can.* If you are convinced you have made Jock understand exactly what he's being punished for — outright defiance to a command — and he's the rough and tough sort, he'll take a terrific beating, figurative or literal, and think the more of you for it. But such dogs, in most breeds, are exceedingly rare.

CHAPTER XVI

Barkers — Good, Bad and Indifferent

Now that we have seen Jock in the role of a dog that persists in barking when you want him to keep still, suppose we cast him as the diametrically opposite type — the kind that persists in keeping still when you want him to bark. It's a great satisfaction to own a sensible levelheaded fellow that doesn't keep you and the neighbors on edge all day or awake half the night, or both, by yelling himself hoarse over nothing at all. Yet there are dogs so ridiculously calm and complacent under all sorts of provocative conditions that people lose all respect for them. The dog that greets the most sinister and suspicious-looking stranger exactly as he does Uncle Joe and Aunt Eliza, who drop in every few days for a call, is bound to be put down as just a big-hearted boob. You may want that kind of dog. If so, you're welcome to him. Most of us like to own one with a little more ability to size up strangers and discriminate between desirables and undesirables, together with a determination to let us know his conclusions. This ability and determination are what make a good watchdog. Possessing these qualities, Jock may be big or little, bold or retiring, and for service inside the house, noisy or almost inarticulate.

The idea that a good watchdog must necessarily be a big bruiser with a deep bass voice, fire in his eye, bristling hair on his shoulders and murder in his heart, is all wrong. As a matter of fact, under most conditions such a guardian of the peace and your property is figuratively, if not literally, a false alarm. Your sneak thief, second-story man or midnight marauder has murder in his heart, too, insofar as your dog is concerned; but he also has something your dog has not and never can have — a pistol in his pocket or a club in his hand to do the murdering with. This means you may lose your dog as well as your silverware and jewelry. For protection against burglars *when some member of the household is at home,* the little Boston terrier that sleeps at the foot of your bed and whines a quiet warning when some intruder is gumshoeing around the premises is often as good as or better than a great Dane chained to a kennel in the yard. The Dane may turn on the heat with a menacing growl or deep-throated bark that is positively hair-raising, only to have his skull bashed in with a club or get a bullet in his brain for his ferocity.

The little Boston's technique makes it possible for you to step quickly to the telephone and call the police. They may very possibly arrive in time to save the silverware, catch the prowler and put him out of circulation for a while.

There are cases, of course, where a really formidable watchdog is necessary. If that is your situation you are likely to find certain breeds much better fitted for the work than others. Doberman pinschers, German shepherds, boxers, mastiffs, great Danes, and so on, are usually natural protectors and can put up a terrific battle with all comers. I say "usually" again to keep you from forgetting that in this respect, as in all others, certain individuals defy all the rules.

But while in all breeds there are isolated individuals who lack true breed character and characteristics, it's the exceptional specimen that doesn't run true to ancestral type. To be reasonably sure you are getting the type you want you must know your pup's ancestry; and in 99 cases out of 100 you can know that only if he or she is a purebred. To quote from a news release sent out by the American Kennel Club:

Essentially, there is nothing wrong with crossbreeding. But it becomes dangerous when the purchaser of a mongrel is not informed of all the details of its breeding. If he knows he is buying a guard dog that comes from a breed or breeds noted for quick use of defensive measures, then he can treat that dog accordingly. But if a dog with such a nature has the outward appearance of a patient house pet, there is trouble ahead for someone.

Continually cases are brought to our attention in which people have purchased from unscrupulous dealers dogs purported to be of certain known and gentle breeds. In appearance these mongrels were similar to certain breeds recognized as purebred. But no one knew absolutely, since they were not registered. Later they developed vicious characteristics that revealed their mixed parentage.

I need only travel two hundred yards from my home to show you a case in point. A neighbor bought as a playmate for his three young children what he was assured was a two-months-old cocker. When he called me over a week or so after his purchase it took but a glance to identify the pup as a mongrel of mongrels; but as almost always happens in such cases, my neighbor took his medicine and kept the dog. The pup grew into a 55-pound, brass-eyed what-is-it with a disposition so mean that the man was only too glad to leave him behind when he moved from town the following summer.

Of course, this principle works both ways. While not in any way dangerous, it is just as disappointing to find a pup sold to you as from fine watchdog stock turning out to be a good-natured slob. Moral: remember you can't tell by the looks of a tadpole how far he'll jump when a frog. If you need a good watchdog, play it as safe as you can and don't waste your money on a crossbred puzzle.

Remember, too, that a good watchdog is *born and made,* with the emphasis pretty evenly distributed. What will tend to make Jock the guardian you hoped for?

We'll first assume he's an indoor dog — a house pet, the same Jock you have taught not to bark his head off every time he hears the doorbell or rush wildly ahead of you when you go to open the door. You have also taught him by the use of the very same system not to bark at any of the everyday sounds in and outside the house that he should know are nothing to be excited about. But there are now and then strange and unusual sounds you *want* him to be excited about; if you could hear them, they might make you a little nervous yourself. How can you induce him to notice them and call them to your attention?

The answer lies in the fact that you can always depend on Jock to take his moods from yours. You taught him to consider the doorbell nothing for him to worry about by making him realize it was an everyday sound and *didn't worry you.* You went further than that and showed him that, when it *did* worry *him,* you considered him not only silly, but a nuisance. Now you hear something that is *not* an everyday sound. You don't know what causes it and for that reason it *does* worry you. All right; let Jock know it does. Stop short, listen intently and in a low but nervous and apprehensive tone say: "Jock! Listen! What is that? Listen!" or something of the sort. To rouse him to still greater tension raise your index finger and hiss two or three times in a sharp staccato. It's a very phlegmatic dog that will not respond to that much stimulus with at least an anxious whine. But if he fails to get the point do a little acting for his benefit. Glance quickly and nervously in all directions, hurry to this place and that, peer under the piano, open a closet door, even look under the rug, keeping up a running fire of talk all the time: "Hunt him up, Jock! Pst, pst! Hunt him up!" etc., etc. If this doesn't eventually break down his sales resistance and bring the barks, I give up and, in my opinion, you might as well give up too.

You may think this method will make trouble for you the next time the doorbell rings. It may; but a few warnings given in your calmest tones and the fact that, as we have said, Jock adapts his moods to yours will be the answer.

To custom-make a watchdog for outdoor work, allow no one but yourself, not even another member of your family, to handle or even feed him. Try to make him what is known as a one-man dog. Use tactics exactly opposite to those that tend to make him socially inclined. By this I mean let him mix with strangers as little as possible. Keep him chained to his kennel, where he can see callers, but has no opportunity to make friends with them.

You can develop his suspicion of visitors by appearing to be suspicious yourself, which, you already realize, is simply a modification of the system we have suggested for the indoor dog.

You might, if driven to it, stage a fake scuffle with a caller. If you do this call to the dog for assistance during your pretended struggle. It's unnecessary to say that if you try this scheme, you must be sure Jock's chain and collar are good and strong and the staple or ring to which the chain is fastened absolutely pull-proof.

In both inside and outside training never forget the invariable words of praise when Jock responds to your efforts with barks, growls or, as in the case of the Boston terrier, warning whines.

You may find your individual dog responds to certain stimuli I have not mentioned. Try to discover what they are. Use your own ingenuity to ring the changes on the stereotyped formula, always remembering our fundamental principle — your dog's moods and actions will be an imitation of yours. Do that and you can regulate Jock's sound effects almost as easily as the man on the movie lot regulates his synthetic thunder and lightning.

CHAPTER XVII

Assault with Intent to Kill

Jock and the family cat are already a pair of pals, but Jock and the cat next door or down the street have developed a feud to rival a couple of West Virginia clans. In this feud the dog was the original aggressor and still is the one that takes the offensive, but the chances are he confines himself strictly to chasing. The cat is usually amply able to protect himself, but that may not prevent your neighbor from making a protest. There are cases, too, where a dog has the real killer instinct and for that reason the average cat cannot take the situation into his own claws.

If Jock is that kind of dog introduce him to a full-grown female with a litter of nursing kittens — and have the arnica and witch hazel handy. If you are obliged to use either or both more than two or three times to treat his wounds, you own a glutton for punishment; and he's probably a terrier. A wirehair, Scottie or almost any member of that group fears nothing on four legs. He will mix it up with a porcupine until his nose fairly bristles with barbed quills, come home with his face looking like an animated hairbrush, and allow his master to torture him with the long and painful pulling-out process without so much as a whimper. He will then go out and pounce on the next porcupine he runs across with undiminished fury and optimism.

Cats are much more common than porcupines, however, and the novelty of heckling them may wear off as days go by and old wounds reopened begin to have a sobering effect. Then, too, a porcupine, when attacked, simply rolls itself into a ball and lies still, thus offering temptation pretty hard to resist. An active tabby with half a dozen kittens to protect packs enough vim, vigor and voltage to give any dog living the shock of his life.

Your own or your neighbor's domestic fowls are a totally different matter. All bird dogs, as well as many other breeds, are natural chicken killers; and nearly all take to eating eggs, once they get a taste of them, like a poor little rich boy to a lollypop. This means you should lose no time in teaching Jock to leave both severely alone. Don't put off this training until he has learned to obey the whistle, behave well on leash or even until he is housebroken. The younger he is the better, if he's only two months. See that his very first acquaintance with hens and chickens is made in your way, not his.

To introduce him properly to barnyard fowls take him out on a long cord instead of a leash, so that he can approach much nearer an unsuspecting hen than you can and feel himself comparatively free. If he is a very small puppy and you can locate a very large rooster or a good big hen with a brood of chicks, the rooster or hen may, like Tabby the cat, take the training business in hand by dashing at the little fellow with flapping wings to give him a good scare. With some pups this is all there is to it; no further training is necessary.

Naturally you can't count on this, so keep a firm hold on the cord and when Jock makes a lunge, yank him back sharply, scolding him with the "No, no!" he may or may not have learned to recognize as meaning "Stop it!" If he hasn't learned that lesson this is a good opportunity to begin teaching it. He will probably be rebellious and persist in pulling, even after a series of yanks. When he does this, don't lose your temper; simply work your way up to him, taking in the cord hand over hand as a fisherman hauls in his line. When you reach him take him by the collar and punish him with a folded newspaper *at the spot where he refused to quit pulling,* scolding him as usual with each blow.

By this time the hen or hens have gotten out of the way. Wait a few minutes to allow them to settle down again, then repeat the routine.

Young pups, like young children, are very impressionable, and if you repeat these lessons every day or so for a week or two, Jock will probably give up resisting the pull on the cord and stand quietly watching the hens or else actually hesitate to go too near them. At that stage you may safely give up holding the cord in your hand, simply allowing it to trail on the ground. If Jock suddenly decides to take another try at chasing, you are in a position to step on the cord and throw him end over end, which is usually much more effective than your original yanks.

Of course a dog thoroughly trained to obey the whistle or call to come in will give you no trouble whatever. I remember a certain bird-dog pup of mine that had never so much as seen a live hen, yet was so instantly obedient to my police whistle that when she was hot on the heels of her first Rhode Island Red, one sharp trill actually sent her sprawling as she desperately slammed on her emergency brakes. That's a little too much to expect, but it shows what training can do.

While on this subject I want to cite a second example of a dog with intelligence enough to understand the *reason* behind an order and to recognize a situation where he could disregard it.

Years ago a spinster who lived near me in the country decided to go in for poultry raising and, as a starter, bought a lot of baby chicks. One day when her Leghorns were about a month old, she put sixty of them in a new wire-enclosed run where there was plenty of fresh green grass. She then called her Airedale, Doc, and the pair rode away in her feeble old Ford to spend the day with a friend in a village eight or ten miles distant. On the return trip the car broke down and it was well after dark before the woman and her dog reached home. To make matters worse, a cold rain had fallen and the would-be chicken raiser suddenly realized her new run contained no coop for shelter.

In a panic, she lit her lantern and hurried out to her chickens. Doc followed; but he had been taught to keep away from feathers and waited outside the run as the worried woman began searching for her chicks. It was very dark, the grass was wet and matted and she realized they must already be dead or too chilled and water-soaked to move.

Suddenly she heard an anxious whine at her side. Despite his training, Doc had jumped the low wire fence and with that never-failing nose of his had located a chicken, lying half-dead under the matted grass, too weak to make a move or sound. You can fill in the rest of the story. I need only say Doc found and picked up every last one of those sixty chicks and a few minutes in a warm oven brought them back to normal again. If he had not decided here was a case where a rule was made to be broken his mistress would have lost more than half her entire flock.

Now back to Jock. If he has had his teeth in a chicken when his anti-chasing training begins, it simply means you must use a little more time and patience. Or you may try the dangerous experiment of cutting open a dead chicken, inserting something supposed to be offensive to a dog, like ipecac or red pepper, and leaving the bird for him to find and attempt to eat. But be sure what you use *is* offensive. Dogs, like the rest of us, sometimes have strange tastes.

A chicken killer that none of the measures we have mentioned will cure means a disagreeable job ahead. Here's the recipe — and it's not a savory dish.

Catch your dog in the act of killing a chicken, even if you have to buy the victim and set the stage for the crime. Habitual killers usually do a snappy job and the bird is either dead or near it when you take it away. If it is dead, so much the better; its fluttering will not excite him. If alive, kill it at once by wringing its neck or pressing steadily and strongly on its body beneath its wings. Now comes the dirty work — and it is dirty. Take the dog firmly by the collar or scruff of the neck and give him a sound thrashing *over the head and face* with the dead chicken, holding it by the legs.

Don't pull your punches and don't let up until the killer's whole head is smeared with blood and other unpleasant things and the chicken pretty well demolished. Then hang the mangled remains to the dog's neck, give him a final tongue-lashing and send him on his malodorous way. Let him carry his badge of disgrace for a day or two if possible. By that time he is pretty sure to lose his desire to kill anything with feathers on it.

This system has been condemned as inhuman and altogether disgusting. So are the gallows, gas chamber and electric chair; but they are still with us. Admitting the last three are supposed (mistakenly, according to statistics) to have a reforming effect on other potential murderers and that the beating with the dead chicken has none, the fact remains that confirmed fowl killers are public enemies. Add to this the fact that the beating described is far less cruel than its only alternative, continuous confinement at the end of a chain, and you may conclude that the end justifies the means.

Grown dogs that attack or kill sheep, cattle, and such, are far less common; but they exist and do much more serious damage. The old-time cure for a sheep killer was to put him in a pen with an ugly old ram and keep him there until he acquired a healthy respect for wool. As a rule this didn't take long; but it is out of the question, of course, for the average dog that stampedes a

flock of sheep or kills a lamb while he and his
owner are enjoying a day's vacation in the country and are out for a stroll through the fields.
For this fellow, as for cattle chasers of all kinds,
try the following.

Get from your butcher a lower leg and hoof of
a sheep or calf, and, without the knowledge of
your dog, lay a trail ending in a shed, barn, garage,
or, better yet, in a thick clump of bushes. Have
a confederate, a stranger to the dog, hide at the
end of the trail. Put the dog on the scent at the
point where you began laying it. When he reaches
the barn, shed or clump of bushes, this confederate
grabs him by the collar and gives him a good beating. Dogs that kill or worry domestic animals are
usually hounds or some other breed that will take
a trail and follow it, paying little or no attention
to where they are going or what their surroundings may be. This makes it easy for the man in
hiding to catch and punish the trailer. This same
plan often works equally well on dogs that chase
deer or other game out of season or in states where
the running of deer by dogs at any time is against
the law. A few beatings of the kind described will
make most hounds give up the idea that deer are
not only fascinating but legitimate quarry.

Now how does all the corporal punishment we
have been advocating jibe with the fact that cat
chasing, sheep and calf killing, deer trailing and

other crimes in that category are admittedly instinctive in certain dogs and even throughout entire breeds? Shouldn't they be considered in Class One, for which corporal punishment is supposed to be taboo? The answer is no. We have already said that in certain cases dogs should be expected to make even their instincts take a back seat to the will of their masters; and the specific acts we have been discussing are cases in point. What's more, dogs that have the instinct to kill almost never appear to resent being punished for it in the sense that their feelings are hurt. I don't attempt to explain this, but I know it is true. And don't overlook the fact that punishment is not used except as a last resort, when milder measures fail. Finally, killers, whether canine or human, are not the type to be easily cowed.

To close this none-too-pleasant chapter, we'll summon to the bar the pup that has learned to eat eggs. To cure him of the habit blow an egg as you used to do years ago when you collected birds' eggs, except that the holes in the shell should be large enough to allow the insertion of a good dose of ipecac, pepper or something of the kind. Close up the holes with wax paper or cellophane and "plant" the egg where Jock will be sure to find it. If this scheme fails to function it will probably be because Jock's nose functions altogether too well.

CHAPTER XVIII

Where Is My Wandering Dog Tonight?

SOME dogs that live in the suburbs or in the country have the social complex so strongly developed they become regular gadabouts. They take half their meals away from home and sometimes even spend the night at the house of a favorite neighbor. This is serious or of no consequence depending on the owner's attitude. Some people seem to feel as much flattered by their dogs' popularity around town as they are by their own.

But it may be you are not keen about having Jock go in for a social career. Much as you may appreciate any successes he seems likely to achieve, you still feel he is your dog, not public property, and prefer to keep him so. You also realize that this constant calling and visiting means he is eating all kinds of food, which is not good for his health, and receiving all kinds of indulgent treatment, which is not good for his training. If you are wise, you have insisted that all his actual education be left to you and you alone. Even the other members of your family have not been allowed to interfere, because such interference is bound to be demoralizing. How much more demoralizing the petting, pampering and indulgence of Tom, Dick and Harry and their respective families can be you realize only too well.

So the sooner you take this case in hand the better. The running-away-from-home habit, if anticipated, is fairly easy to prevent, but once it has become well fixed it is a stickler. Begin by keeping an eye on Jock when he is playing outdoors, and the minute he shows an inclination to wander over into the next yard or out into the street, call him back. If he is obstinate and tries it again, be patient enough to repeat your calls or whistles each time he reaches the boundary. After four or five attempts on his part and recalls on yours, simply tie him up at his kennel or put him back in the house. After a few days of this he will probably catch the idea and be inclined to stick around. If, later on, you catch him in the act of making a getaway and feel a little punishment would do him good, remember the old rule: punish him at the point where he committed his fault — in this case at the boundary line he is not to overstep.

The cure of a runaway is much more difficult when your dog has another dog to play with — that of a neighbor, for instance. Two dogs will stray away when either, by itself, would stay at home. This is particularly true of the sporting breeds in a locality where they can easily reach hunting territory. The two pals may have no definite intention of breaking the rules. As they are playing one runs ahead of the other, the latter hurries along to catch and pass his playmate and become the leader in his turn. Before either really realizes it, the pair are off on an extended hunting trip. The same thing is true, to a lesser extent, of all the active breeds. When this happens you and your neighbor should be able to arrange things in such a way that the two victims of the wanderlust are not at liberty at the same times.

Now we'll say you have neglected this early training and suddenly realize you have a habitual tramp on your hands. Instead of preventing your dog from becoming a runaway you must reform an old offender. Some say that underfeeding will cure the habit. Their theory is that a short absence from home and the feed pan will bring the pangs of hunger and the dog will hurry back to get something to eat. My own experience has indicated the exact opposite is more often the case and for two reasons. A hungry dog is far more likely to wander from home than a well-fed one in the first place, and once he is out on a foraging expedition will spend hours investigating every open garbage can within the radius of a mile before he will give up and make tracks for his kennel and supper. For, strange as it may seem, your very aristocrat of aristocrats, fed on the finest of food, often seems to prefer the most evil-smelling messes he can find.

A much better plan, in my opinion, is to use the broom-handle system you tried with success, I hope, when Jock began chasing automobiles. Tie the stick to his collar every time you allow him outdoors by himself. Few dogs will travel far when hampered in that way, and even if they do are easily caught by anyone who sees them. If your name and address are stamped on Jock's collar plate, the truant will almost invariably be returned promptly by the party who picked him up or held incommunicado until you can be notified to come and get your dog.

Under no circumstances inflict physical punishment on the wanderer that comes home of his own accord, no matter how long he has been away or how great the temptation may be. If the dog knows why he is being whipped, which is very unlikely, he will stay away still longer the next time, to put off the spanking he knows he's going to get when he reaches home. If he doesn't know why he is whipped, a hiding will merely mystify him and do more harm than good.

On the other hand to kill the fatted calf by making a fuss over him is almost as bad. The wisest plan is to receive him with cool indifference, chain him up at his kennel and leave him there to think it over. You can also go back to first principles and use for a week or so the system we described to prevent the formation of the runaway habit — watchful waiting when Jock is at liberty and punishment when and if he oversteps the boundary line.

While all we have said about making neighborhood calls, accepting invitations to dinner, deliberate and unpremeditated straying away, and so on, relates more especially to suburban and country residents and their dogs, the suggestions given may be helpful to city dwellers who take their dogs to the country for long vacations or who have summer places in rural sections.

Wherever you live — in city, suburbs or country — there is one phase of the runaway problem that is really serious. This is the possibility that your dog may be stolen or become confused and unable to find his way home. The latter sometimes happens when the dog is not a runaway at all, but is simply out with you for a walk. In such cases you and he become separated and neither of you is able to locate the other. Whatever the cause, the dog may be picked up and appropriated by someone who knows a high-class purebred when he sees one, or may simply stray away and become hopelessly lost.

This is easily possible in heavy city traffic. But it seldom happens if the dog belongs to one of the sporting breeds. Incredible as it seems, most gun dogs or hounds can unravel an owner's track in the maze of footprints on a sidewalk used by hundreds of people during every five minutes. But these breeds are trailing specialists, and the chances are Jock has no such ability, nor the instinct to use it if he has. If you and he are unfortunate enough to lose each other in this way, go back to the last place where you and he were together. He is pretty sure to go back there too. If you and he spent ten minutes in a certain shop, visit it. You may find him waiting for you.

There is nothing you can do about a stolen dog except to report the theft to the police, which you should also do when you believe his failure to come back to you or to his kennel is as serious to him as it is to you.

Dogs taken to unfamiliar woods or fields in the country sometimes lose their bearings and may never find their way home without assistance. This frequently happens with a hound that has been carried to some distant hunting ground in a car. He picks up and follows a fox or deer track for hours until he is miles out of sight or hearing, and his owner is finally forced by darkness or some other reason to drive home and leave his dog behind.

If the owner knows his business he will locate the place where he and his dog were last together and leave there something that carries his own personal scent, like his glove or shooting coat. When the hound drives his fox to earth or the deer runs him so ragged he quits the chase, he will invariably pick up his own trail and backtrack, with the idea that this will lead him home or to the huntsman. When he reaches the glove or coat, he feels his master is somewhere near and waits there or close by for him to appear even if it means overnight or longer.

Of course this would not be true if both man and dog had not originally come to the region in a car. If they had started out from home on foot, the hound would never be lost. Though many miles from his kennel and in country absolutely strange to him, he would backtrack the whole distance, if it took him forty-eight hours or more to make the trip.

If Jock is not that kind of trailer and you and he lose each other in unfamiliar surroundings in the country, you can try a modification of this scheme with equal or even greater chances of success. You will not be obliged to go home and leave the wanderer in the woods because non-sporting breeds seldom travel long or far before realizing they have become separated from their master and hurrying back to the spot where they saw him last. So instead of starting out to hunt for Jock simply sit down and let him hunt for you. Whistle and call every few minutes and you'll be pretty sure to find he is a much cleverer G-man than you are.

If for any reason it is absolutely impossible to wait a reasonable length of time, take the fox hunter's tip, leave your glove or handkerchief and return to the place as soon as you can. Jock may hear you coming and come running to meet you before you reach the spot where you and he parted company. If not, he's almost certain to be within calling distance or to come within calling distance before long. So keep moving slowly about to make it easy for him to discover you. And don't forget he knows the old song, "Whistle an' I'll come to ye, me darlin'," and in all probability is hoping you know it too, and will follow the good advice it gives.

CHAPTER XIX

When Jock Goes to College

Up to this point we have confined ourselves fairly closely to what all well-mannered dogs should do and not do — the everyday etiquette that in people indicates what we call good breeding. These essentials any dog can learn and almost any owner can teach. Certain professionals with an axe to grind and a living to make may tell you otherwise, but don't believe that sort of buncombe. Training Jock to lie quietly at your feet or not to jump up and put his paws on visitors requires no mumbo jumbo.

A moss-grown maxim among handlers has it that, to train a dog, you must know more than the dog does; but that doesn't tell the whole story. You may know a thousand times as much as your dog, yet be unwilling to take the trouble or lack the time and patience to put your knowledge to good use. Perhaps you are a very busy person with little spare time or perhaps you are very nervous and high-strung or very unobservant. People have even been known to be as careless or indifferent about the education of their dogs as they sometimes

are about more important things — the education
of their children, for instance. But whatever your
circumstances, disposition or inclinations, you have
sufficient time and ability to teach Jock four simple
things; and for your own reputation, that of your
dog, and for the good name of dogs in general, I
beg you to do it. These four fundamentals are: to
obey your whistle or call; to be cleanly in your
own house or the houses of your friends; not to
welcome visitors by jumping all over them, and
to behave in such a way in your car that you can
invite a friend for a ride without subjecting your
passenger to constant mauling and general dis-
comfort. You are fairly successful in obeying ten
commandments in regard to your own conduct;
you should be able to obey only four for regulating
the conduct of your dog.

I hope you aim much higher than that; that
you have learned to enjoy giving Jock his lessons,
have gotten a thrill out of his response to your
training and are properly proud of the fact that
he is in every way a canine gentleman. If that is
your attitude you have probably reached a point
where you would like to see him not only a gentleman but an accomplished one. This means you
may decide to pit him against other accomplished
dogs in officially recognized obedience tests at the
shows, or to give him a college education in certain more or less difficult tricks he will perform

for the benefit of your friends and acquaintances.

When you do either or both of these things, you will be surprised to learn how easily you can impress the public with your own and your dog's cleverness. It's like Mr. Cass with his two setters walking at heel.

Assuming that Jock is letter-perfect in the comparatively few details of correct deportment already discussed in this book, you have only to adapt them to obedience-test conditions, add two or three more to comply with special requirements, and you have a candidate for public competition. This will be treated a little more fully in the next chapter.

In trick work, you will have almost unlimited opportunity to exercise your own individual ingenuity and the *native* as well as the acquired ability of your dog. You notice "native" is in italics. This is because you have had ample time to study Jock's individual mental and physical characteristics and you can make them play right into your hand when you choose the various stunts you plan for his program. But you should also consider his physical adaptability for any given trick you have in mind. Certain dogs are far more agile and muscular for their weight and inches than others. Some, again, have peculiar and amusing eccentricities or habits that you can exploit to win applause.

I remember a little Boston terrier that would cry like a baby when told his master had lost a lot of money in the market or that his playmate, the pussy, was sick. The tears ran down his cheeks in streams and he made a gurgling sound not unlike the sobs of a child. How he had been taught this trick was a mystery to me at the time. I know now that there is an occasional perfectly healthy dog whose eyes, under certain conditions, distill water like a retort. The Boston's master noticed he had that peculiarity and cashed in on it.

Jock may have no such spectacular gift, but he is bound to have *some* characteristics peculiar to himself. Watch for these and other straws that show which way his mental and physical breezes blow and turn them to account. A very common straw of this kind is the pleasure most dogs derive from chasing and picking up thrown articles, and the natural inclination to bring them back to the thrower to be tossed out again. These two perfectly normal traits are responsible for the talented tyke that goes to the door when the postman rings, gets the morning mail and delivers it to his master at the breakfast table or in the library. They also explain the gallantry of the dog that carries a bundle or basket of groceries for his mistress when he and she go shopping together.

BUT — and it's a good big "but" — instinct, inclination and physical adaptability, while pennies from Heaven as a basis for successful instruction in trick work, are frequently rank counterfeits unless supplemented by strict and very thorough training. For they are a very uncertain quantity and the trainer who depends on them for results is very likely to be thrown for a loss when at a critical moment his temperamental star decides he's not in the mood to go through with his act. Trick dogs should be taught to be good "troupers" and that the play must go on whether or no they feel like giving a performance. So, without discounting the value of Jock's enthusiasm over performing some clever trick, remember that while it is a great asset, your insistence that he *invariably* do that trick at your command is a still greater one.

At the same time don't allow your pupil to lose this natural enthusiasm through too long training sessions, too severe methods of discipline or any similar lack of tact in your teaching. Avoid these pitfalls and your dog will not only give an artistic performance; he will show a true artist's pride and pleasure in giving it.

This is vital to success. No one can predict the kind of reception a human actor or actress will get from an audience; but the performance of a trained animal — horse, dog, parrot, seal or what-have-you — is almost invariably received in the spirit in which it is given. The next time you see a "dog act" on the stage or sit at the ringside watching an obedience test, notice the applause for the dog that does his work with a merrily wagging tail. No dog wags his tail unless he's having a good time — no amount of training can make him do it. The spectators know this and appreciate his good nature and his evident enjoyment of his work. It's unnecessary to ask them to give the clever little dog a great big hand; they do it spontaneously.

The same thing is true of dogs that are being put through their paces and posed in the show ring to be judged for conformation, soundness, condition, and so forth, in competition for bench honors. Wagging tails are as infectious there as everywhere else, and even judges are influenced by them sometimes.

Since you expect Jock to be a good showman, you must be a good showman too. For example, you will learn in the next chapter how to teach Jock to search for, find and bring to you some familiar object like a ball or an old glove and to "speak" on signal. For trick purposes you will substitute for the ball or glove your cane or umbrella or Jock's leash and develop the two perfectly simple acts into a much more elaborate routine. When your audience is duly seated you call Jock to you and talk to him exactly as you would to your child of fourteen, using a quiet conversational tone.

You say something like this perhaps:

"Now, Jock, sit down and listen to me very closely because there is something I want you to do for me, if you will. I left your leash on the floor in the southeast corner of my bedroom next the little table with the electric lamp on it. We shall want it when we take our little stroll in the park, don't you think so?"

Jock barks "Yes" enthusiastically.

"Very well then, you might as well save me the trouble of climbing the stairs, isn't that right?"

Again Jock barks his agreement.

"Good. I thought you'd be glad to be of service. You like to do things for me, don't you?"

Another bark from Jock.

"Fine! You're a good dog. Remember now — your leash on the floor in the southeast corner of my bedroom next the little table with the electric lamp on it. Do you understand?"

More barks.

"All right, go on up and fetch it down."

When Jock does exactly as he's told, your visitors may be amazed at his knowledge of the English language. Yet he actually recognizes only four words during your whole "conversation" — sit, leash, bedroom, and fetch, all of which you have mildly emphasized in talking to him. These and the "speak" signal are all the stage direction he needs, but the more elaborate your spiel the more effective the act, as in the case of the sleight-of-hand artist who takes the rabbit out of his hat.

For me to suggest any specific stunts you should select for Jock's repertory is not only unnecessary, it would be presumptuous. The chances are your imagination is much livelier than mine; and what's more to the point, *I don't know Jock. You do* — or should. If you don't and he doesn't know you, this book has failed of its purpose.

CHAPTER XX

Training for Obedience Tests

As you already know, obedience tests conducted according to rules and regulations drawn up by the American Kennel Club have not only become tremendously popular with dog owners, they are also a smashing hit with the public that helps make dog shows possible. The dog that wins successively the titles C.D. (Companion Dog), C.D.X. (Companion Dog Excellent), and U.D. (Utility Dog) richly deserves the points, ribbons and reputation he gets, and to be awarded even a C.D. is no mean honor. For nowadays competition is keen and standards are high.

Sometimes these trials are held by clubs that specialize in this feature and are not in any way connected with a bench show proper. But if points toward a title are to be won these events must be licensed by the Kennel Club and all the rules and regulations complied with. These requirements, which define correct conduct of a show, eligibility of handlers, dogs, and so forth, you may learn by applying to the American Kennel Club, 221 Fourth Avenue, New York City.

For the purposes of this book it is enough for you to know the routine necessary to win the various titles we have mentioned and to learn a little something about preparing Jock to go through them with credit to you and to himself. We'll take them in order.

The tests in the Novice Classes are: (1) To heel on leash. (2) To heel free. (3) To come when called. (4) To sit for a period of one minute away from handler. (5) To lie down for three minutes away from handler. Points won in these classes count toward the title C.D.

A perfect performance counts 100 points. When Jock has scored 85 points at each of three trials in which six or more dogs compete in the Novice Classes, he wins the coveted C.D.

Presumably you have already taught Jock every one of the requirements, so you can devote your time to perfecting his technique. But perfect technique as set down in the Kennel Club rules may call for a little more instruction than you have given. "To heel on leash," for example, sounds simple; but let me quote from the official interpretation of that test.

While in the act of walking at heel the judge will repeatedly give the order "Halt." At each such order "the handler will stop and his dog immediately should sit without command at heel and not move until ordered to do so. It is permissible after each halt, before moving again, for the handler to give the order 'Heel' to his dog. Any tightening or jerking of the leash or any act, signal or command which in the opinion of the Judges gives the dog unnecessary or unfair assistance shall be penalized. The Judge will give the orders 'Left turn,' 'Right turn,' 'About turn,' 'Slow' and 'Double,' which last order signifies the handler must run. . . . The Judge will order the handler to execute the 'Figure Eight,' which signifies that the handler shall walk around and in between the two stewards, who shall stand not more than eight feet apart, or if there is only one steward shall walk around and in between the Judge and the steward."

This looks pretty formidable, but when you come to analyze it, all you need do is teach Jock to sit when you stop walking, rise to the order "Heel" when you resume your walk, run when you do and make the turns neatly without leaving his proper place at your side. I have an idea that if someone had given our old friend Cass that assignment, he would have crashed through in a week or so, handling two dogs instead of one. To teach Jock to do the left turn correctly use your leash and left leg, the leg nudging him to let him know the direction to take. If he runs too far ahead he will probably be brought up sharply by the leash and realize it is the result of his own mistake. The leash will jerk him back, too, if he fails to notice you are making a right turn, and he will readily learn to be on the watch for any sudden changes of direction you may make. This, of course, is assuming that he already sits and comes to heel promptly on command and stays put in either case. You will probably rely on the jerk of your leash, too, to accustom Jock to sudden stops on your part and to teach him not to be caught napping when they occur. As in your original heeling lessons you will be able to dispense with the leash when the dog gets the idea that he is to look

USING LEG TO TEACH
LEFT TURN; LEASH IN
WRONG HAND

alive at all times and hold his position at your left side. The Figure Eight, you readily see, is simply a combination of right and left turns; but you will need the help of two friends or members of your family to make Jock understand exactly what he is to do in the ring.

Which reminds me that in many of the obedience-test stunts the ring may be full of dogs and their handlers, and that you must accustom Jock to perform under those conditions with no evidences of stage fright. If you make inquiries you will probably find there are obedience-test clubs in your vicinity and they will be glad to have you join the group classes they offer. Whether or not there is such a club available, write to the American Kennel Club for their little pamphlet, *Regulations and Standard for Obedience Test Trials.* Study it carefully. Then attend several bench shows that list obedience tests on their program and watch every move made by Judges, stewards, handlers and dogs while they are in the ring. It will be not only interesting but vastly instructive. It will also give you the "feel" of the whole performance and make you much less nervous and self-conscious when the great day comes and you take Jock into the ring for his first test.

The curtain now falls for ten seconds to indicate the passing of — well, maybe ten weeks. Probably it's much less than that. At any rate, you can now write the letters "C.D." after Jock's name and he is eligible to compete in the Open Classes for the title C.D.X. Here he will be expected to: (1) Heel on leash. (2) Heel free. (3) Drop on recall. (4) Retrieve dumbbell on flat. (5) Retrieve dumbbell over obstacle. (6) Make a long jump. (7) Sit for a period of three minutes. (8) Lie down for a period of five minutes.

In these classes a perfect performance counts

250 points. As this is written, a dog acquires his C.D.X. when he has scored 220 or more points in each of three trials at which the competitors in the Open Classes number six or more; but this is subject to change at any time by the American Kennel Club. That, however, is of minor importance to you or me. It's the rules for work in the ring that interest us.

The only new requirements here are to retrieve a dumbbell on the flat and over an obstacle and to negotiate what is called "a long jump." For to drop on recall is simply our old order "Down!" given and obeyed while Jock is coming to you at command. On command again, he rises and comes nearer, when the Judge may require him to repeat the maneuver once more or oftener, as he sees fit. You can easily adapt Jock's present response to this order to these test conditions.

Retrieving a dumbbell over an obstacle calls for entirely new lessons. Jock must be taught to jump for distance and height and also to pick up and bring to you a specific object. The size and weight of the dumbbell are prescribed in the rules as follows: for all dogs except the smaller breeds sixteen ounces, and for the smaller breeds eight ounces. For the high-jumping tests the obstacle must be three and a half feet high for all the large breeds, with the exception of very heavily built dogs like Newfoundlands, Saint Bernards, Great

Pyrenees, and such, which are required to clear but two feet. Small breeds, like dachshunde, small terriers, beagles and toys, must clear an obstacle twice their own height at the shoulder.

The distance for broad jumping varies from four to six feet according to the size of the dog, but for all breeds the obstacle is ten inches in height at its highest point. Since the training required for the jumping tests is much simpler than that for correct form in retrieving the dumbbell, we'll consider that first.

Begin as such training must always begin, whether for horses, dogs or human athletes, with a jump so low it is easily cleared. This will accomplish three things: give Jock confidence, allow you to concentrate on teaching him what he is expected to do and stimulate the natural fondness for jumping which is a characteristic of nearly all breeds. This natural fondness, as we have already learned, is an asset if properly used, and a liability if it is not. It will make Jock give an inspiring performance if he is taught it is a requirement and not simply good fun. Or it will make him refuse to give any performance at all if he is only half trained and doesn't happen to be in the mood.

So let's go. With Jock on a leash you simply walk briskly toward your twelve-inch hurdle, stepping over it when you reach it, at the same time saying "Hop!" in a crisp cheery tone. It's ten to one Jock will jump over the bar. Praise him and repeat the routine until Jock has the jumping idea firmly fixed in his mind, never forgetting the command "Hop!" or the word or two of praise that follows his jump. You see now why the excellent command "Hup!" you may have used for the command to sit proves a bit embarrassing at this stage. Even so, it's nothing serious. Shakespeare used over 50,000 words, they say, and you should be able to find something besides "Hop" to fit the situation.

When Jock takes the hurdle cleanly every time, alter your own routine by *not stepping over the hurdle* as you and Jock reach it. You and he are now on opposite sides of the obstacle and in all probability he will quickly jump back to your side when you call "Hop!" If he is a good big dog you will probably find a fairly long cord is better than your leash for the jumping lessons as that will obviate any possible jerking when he takes a longer leap than you expected.

The fact that Jock probably enjoys the whole performance as much as you do may make him so eager to jump he will get to the hurdle first, jump it ahead of you and, unless you let go the leash, get a sharp twist of the neck. This is dangerous. To make the jump with a dangling leash may mean all kinds of trouble, and if Jock is the sensi-

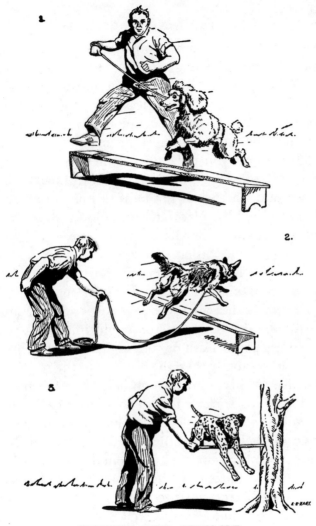

JUMPING OVER OBSTACLE

1. Stepping Over with Dog, on Leash
2. Let Dog Go Over Alone, Still on Leash, or Cord
*3. Raise Stick to Desired Height when Dog Has Mastered
    Jumping without Leash*

tive sort may set him against the whole jumping
proposition. The long cord will be your ace in the
hole, as you can see. But you must avoid the
necessity of using either leash or cord later on,
so you might as well plan for it now. Vary your
routine by stopping short or making a left or
right turn as you walk toward the hurdle, ordering Jock to heel as you do so. This will make him
uncertain whether or not he is to jump at all and
he will hold his place at your side until you are
near enough the hurdle to give the order "Hop!"
Also give the order "Down!" when Jock has
cleared his hurdle to prevent him from jumping
back again without waiting for your command.

When he has all this down pat — and I doubt
if it will take as long as you might imagine — you
can forget your leash or cord and, when you think
it wise, gradually raise the obstacle to the required
height. At this point you can help things along by
using a long stick or broom handle instead of the
hurdle, holding one end tightly against a post or
tree and holding the other end in your hand. But
be sure to keep the stick horizontal. The stick has
another advantage besides its handiness: it makes
Jock understand he is to *jump over* an object he
could *duck under* just as well. Keep on ordering
him to "down" after each jump before leaping
back to the other side again. Then he will be
constantly under your control. And don't forget

the kind words and pats on the head when he does his work well.

To teach the broad jump the system is practically the same. Begin with a jump of not more than two feet, which, as in stepping over the hurdle, you take with the dog. Use the leash or cord as you did in the high-jumping lessons, and as an added precaution set the obstacle at right angles to a wall or the side of a building and tightly against it. When Jock jumps the full four or six feet required for his breed without either leash or cord, it is only a matter of perfecting his form. If he is sloppy about clearing the distance cleanly over the broad-jump obstacle or the high-jump hurdle do as is done at the horse-racing tracks — put a little brush from one of your small shrubs on the barrier. Jock will not fancy the feel of it if he is lazy or careless and will try to make his jumps good and clean.

The directions given here for teaching high and broad jumping cover the fundamentals, but you will learn much for yourself by working with Jock, watching the tests at the shows, talking with judges and exhibitors and by studying the requirements as set down in the Kennel Club pamphlet already mentioned. A fair-sized book might be written on training for obedience-test work alone. The suggestions I have offered will give both you and Jock a start in the right direction, however, and, if you happen to have a natural flair for training, you may even discover ways to modify and improve them.

Now for the next chapter and something a little more difficult — teaching Jock to retrieve.

CHAPTER XXI

Training for Obedience Tests
(Continued)

THE LOVE for retrieving is, like the love of jumping, almost always inborn in dogs, and is both a liability and an asset. In all probability Jock already gets a big kick out of chasing a thrown ball and bringing it back to you on the run, so that you can throw it for him again. But he does this *only when he happens to feel like it and until the game begins to pall.* He must be taught to take it seriously, as he now takes his jumping act.

To do this select a spot as secluded as possible and use it as a permanent training place. Jock will soon learn to consider it a schoolroom rather than a playground and expect to stick to his lessons when you take him there.

Now order him to sit and take from your pocket some object he can carry easily, like a soft ball, an old glove or the like. One very successful professional trainer advises a corncob, since it is light, easily held in the mouth and can be broken to any desired size; another suggests a piece of rubber hose. Whatever you choose, rub it in your hands thoroughly so that it carries your individual scent. This is important because, when you throw it, Jock must be able to distinguish it from anything similar in appearance he may run across when hunting for it and because it *means more to him because it is yours.*

A farmer neighbor of mine used to pick up an apple from hundreds on the ground under a tree, rub it in his hands, throw it back under the tree and order his cow dog to fetch it. It was interesting to watch that half-breed hunt through those hundreds of Baldwins or McIntoshes, all alike as two peas, until his nose told him he had found the one apple his master had thrown. Any smart dog would do the same, but here's something about that same dog worth pasting in your hat because it is typical of all dogs and so is used in obedience tests.

If anyone but his master threw an apple for this dog in exactly the same way, he would dash for the tree, nose about among the apples a few moments as a bluff, *then bring any apple he happened to pick up.* The scent of his master's hand on that one Baldwin made it different from all other Baldwins. Other people's hands had no such significance. This universal dog characteristic is the origin of the official test that requires a dog to "exercise scent discrimination," a stunt we shall mention again later.

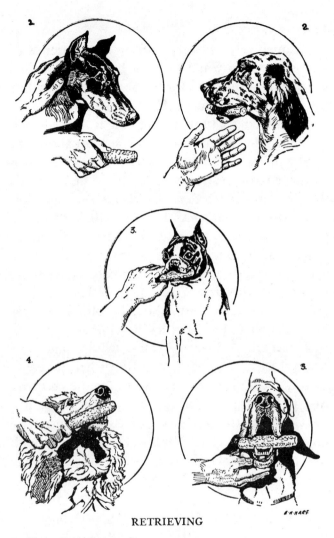

RETRIEVING

1. *Show Dog Corncob*
2. *Call or Whistle Him to You*
3. *Press Corncob against Teeth and Say "Fetch!"*
4. *Continue Pressure till He Stops Resisting Corncob*
5. *Prevent Chewing or Dropping*

Meanwhile Jock is still sitting like patience on a monument so you'd best get back to him. Give him a pat on the head for his obedience, show him the corncob, let him sniff at it to make sure it's yours and make a bluff at throwing it. The chances are he will be instantly alert, sense sport ahead and maybe jump to his feet prepared to chase the corncob when you really toss it away. If he does this, stop feinting and order him to sit. But right here you must be very tactful or he will become disgusted and lose interest. Don't keep him waiting long. Watch your chance, catch him when he is sitting correctly and throw the cob, at the same time giving the order "Go on, Jock! Fetch!"

If he's like most pups he'll be off like a shot, find the cob and either pick it up or start playing with it. If he picks it up, call or whistle and he is pretty likely to bring it with him when he comes to you. Order him to sit as you take the cob from his mouth or as you go and get it, as the case may be. Continue this game as long as Jock thoroughly enjoys it, but never let him start for the cob without your order. He is having a lot of fun, but he must never be allowed to forget he must abide by the rules.

Now we'll assume Jock is the one pup in a hundred that takes little or no interest in the cob or your throwing of it. In some ways that is so much the better. The whole routine is then serious business from the start; yet later on, when he learns the practical purposes to which it can be put, he will take as much pleasure in doing it as if he had enjoyed it from the first. For the present, however, since he isn't interested in your feint tosses and doesn't move when you actually throw the cob, cut out the preliminaries and get right down to business.

Order Jock to sit, put on his leash, praise him a little to put him in good humor, hold the cob close to his muzzle, press it against his teeth and give the order "Fetch!" The chances are he will take the hint and grab the cob. If he doesn't, wait until he opens his mouth to breathe or open it yourself by taking his lower jaw in your hand; then insert the cob and hold his jaws together for a moment, repeating the command "Fetch." Don't be rough about this but keep the pressure on his jaws until he stops resisting it. If he grabs the cob of his own accord he may begin to chew it or drop it almost as soon as it is in his mouth. In that case use the same pressure around his muzzle to prevent his doing either one. Then say "Give it!" or some similar command, release the pressure on his jaws and take the cob in your other hand when he opens his mouth to drop it.

Now pat him on the head, tell him he's a good dog, take him for a little walk of a hundred feet or so and, if he shows the slightest sign of boredom,

play with him a moment or two. Then bring
him back to the original spot and go through the
routine again. Make the sessions short — not more
than ten or fifteen minutes each — and in a day or
two Jock will probably take the cob when you
say "Fetch!" and sit holding it until "Give it!",
when he will deliver it into your hands.

There are at least two possible complications.
Jock may so thoroughly disapprove of the whole
idea that he will not allow you to get the cob close
enough to his nose to slip it into his mouth when
he opens it or you open it for him. That's where
the leash comes in. Hold the cob in your left hand,
take the leash in your right, and pull the dog's
head steadily upward to meet the cob. Be very cool
and firm about this, pulling hard and steadily
enough to make the tightening noose very uncomfortable. Incidentally, the choking effect of the
leash may make Jock open his mouth enough to
make the introduction of the cob easy. But again
the warning — don't be rough about it. Once
the cob is in his mouth and you have a grip
on his muzzle to keep it there, let up on the
leash entirely or enough so that it is no longer
uncomfortable.

The second complication may be that Jock resists giving up the cob instead of wanting to be
rid of it. This brings you back to your other Jock,
who was quite willing to take the cob in his mouth.

1. *Use Leash if He Refuses to Take Corncob*
2. *Pinch Dog's Ear if He Won't Give Up Corncob*
3. *Walking at Heel after Complications Are Corrected*
4. *Retrieving and **Jumping** at Same Time*

He, too, may not like the idea of giving it up, so we can now consider the two hypothetical dogs as one and the same, and you can proceed with your training. A comparatively few sessions have given you a dog that takes the cob from your hand at the command "Fetch!" and holds it in his mouth until you give the order "Give it!", which he is not inclined to obey.

Here is a situation where you will allow no fooling. The moment you start pulling at the cob Jock will pull too, and in a twinkling the two of you are playing a game. That will never do, yet Jock must be forced to obey your command "Give it!" promptly and without any fuss. For the first time since you began your lessons for obedience-test work, you are dealing with a Class Two case in which Jock cannot help knowing what you want him to do but doesn't choose to do it. So a little mild punishment is called for. Give it by pinching Jock's ear just enough to hurt a little, squeezing his front paw or putting your foot on one of his front or rear feet, just as you pressed his rear toes with your shoe when you taught him not to put his paws on your white flannel trousers nearly a year ago. One of these devices is sure to work and you must be sure to give the order "Give it!" as you inflict the punishment and praise Jock when he opens his mouth and you take the cob.

Once this lesson is thoroughly learned it will be easy to teach the dog to come to heel with the cob in his mouth and stand at your side. Now say "Heel!" again and walk a little way, gradually increasing the distance until he will carry the cob as long as he is walking at heel. Stop frequently, order Jock to sit, say "Give it!", take the cob from his mouth, praise him, then repeat the whole routine, always using the commands "Sit!", "Fetch!", "Give it!", and "Heel!" as required.

Now substitute various articles for the corncob, among them the dumbbell you will use in obedience tests. This is a good time to make the change because the dumbbell is very easily picked up from the ground, and that is Jock's next job. You may have absolutely no difficulty in getting him to do this when you put it on the ground in front of him and give the order "Fetch!" On the other hand it may be necessary to press his head down gently, hold it in position with one hand, give the order "Fetch!" and repeat the routine you used when he was in the sitting position. If so, you have had plenty of practice and so has Jock.

When he will pick up the dumbbell at your command and hold it in his mouth as he walks at heel, you may begin throwing it for him to bring back to you. If he doesn't catch the idea immediately and stays in the "sit" position when you give the command "Fetch!", add the encouraging cluck he knows so well and run forward a little way to get him started. Or, if necessary, you can go all the way and pretend to be hunting for the dumbbell. It's a very exceptional dog that will not try to help you when the dumbbell is in plain sight and you repeat the order "Fetch!" Whatever happens be sure he obeys every command you give, even if you have to go through the training for it all over again.

If you stick to this schooling conscientiously and patiently Jock will soon go through the routine required for his obedience test, which is this:

The orders given by the Judge should be "Throw it," whereupon the handler throws the dumbbell; "Send him," whereupon the handler sends his dog to retrieve; "Take it," whereupon the handler takes dumbbell from dog; "Finish," whereupon the handler gives the order to heel.

You will not forget, of course, to teach Jock to bring his dumbbell to you when he must take a jump in the act of doing so. This is easily done, since it is simply a combination of two stunts he has already learned to do and do well: retrieve the dumbbell on command and deliver it properly into your hand. Teach him, too, to search for the thrown dumbbell when it is not in plain sight. If he does not use his eyes or nose to locate it when you cluck and give him the order "Fetch!" go with him as before and begin hunting with him. He'll catch on in one or two lessons at most.

That's the story, and, as in the jumping tests, you will learn a great deal from watching actual competition at the shows.

The curtain falls again to indicate the passing of more time, then rises for Act Three. Jock is now a Companion Dog Excellent, since he has met all the requirements at three sizable shows and come through with his flag flying. Now for top honors — the title "Utility Dog."

Turning to your little pamphlet once more, you will find he will now be asked to speak at command, exercise scent discrimination, seek back for lost articles and stand for examination. This at the show. Then, after he has passed a "tracking test" in open country under the eyes of a Judge approved by the Club for this special occasion, the title U.D. is his — he will be, at long last, a Utility Dog, and both you and he will have a right to be proud of it. With that goal in sight, back to work.

Teaching Jock to speak at command will probably be simple. You can easily tease him into barking by offering him a tidbit and pulling it away when he starts to take it. This has been condemned as unorthodox. Maybe it is, but with most dogs it works well and does no harm, since the victim is always rewarded in the end by getting his tidbit and a pat on the head. But don't try it with a young puppy of uncertain disposition; it's perfectly true that teasing in general is bad medicine. It may make a puppy permanently unreliable and even definitely mean, as well as shake his confidence in you, personally, which is fatal.

Playing a piano will sometimes make a dog bark, so try it. You can often "kid" a dog into speaking simply by talking excitedly to him and arousing his interest or intense curiosity in something you show him or ask him to find for you. Or you may decide to be an opportunist and take advantage of times when he barks of his own accord by reason of some stimulus entirely foreign to anything you have done. In any case, seize the opportunity to give the order "Speak!" when he barks and to praise him extravagantly. You may also resort to the old tidbit system if necessary. No two dogs are temperamentally alike. What will work with one may be no earthly use with another, but one or more of the stratagems suggested will be successful. When Jock learns "Speak!" or "Jock! Speak!" means you want him to bark, the battle is won. In his test he will "speak" from the sitting, standing and down position, the last when you are at least fifteen feet away. So take care of that in your training.

The next two tests are modifications of the act of retrieving and for that reason comparatively little additional training is necessary. What Jock needs now is a *naturally keen nose*. If he has it, well and good; if he lacks it no amount of training can ever fit him for either the scent-discrimination or tracking tests. It may be for this reason, or simply because the average owner cannot see the practical advantages of either requirement, that the title "Utility Dog" is so seldom sought and still more seldom won. During the first four years of obedience-test competition in the United States, hundreds of dogs were awarded the coveted letters C.D. and C.D.X. For the same four years the theoretically much-to-be-desired U.D. was won by exactly thirteen. It goes without saying that many more could have been successful *if their owners had been sufficiently interested to make a bid for it*.

If Jock happens to be a sporting dog he is pretty sure to be equipped by nature for success at both scenting and trailing. If he is a toy or even one of the larger non-sporting breeds, it's a tossup and you should try him out by some such method as that used by our farmer friend with his half-breed dog and Baldwin apples. Assuming you find Jock a likely prospect, here are the official requirements he must meet, exactly as set down in the rules:

Scent discrimination should be exercised on three articles belonging to handler. This test should be repeated three times, testing a different article belonging to handler each time, which shall be placed amongst (but not covered by) several other articles. One article used to be a metal object. Handkerchiefs must not be used. The stranger's article, put down for this exercise, should resemble the handler's article. The handler shall place his object upon the Judge's judging chart [so that it receives no scent from the Judge's hand] and the Judge in turn will drop it amongst the other articles without touching it. The handler meanwhile shall stand so as to block the dog's view.

In seeking back for lost article "the article used must be approved by the Judge and must not be a conspicuous one or white in color. The article used shall be dropped surreptitiously by the handler as he is walking with his dog at heel. After the handler has proceeded at least 30 paces from the place where the article was dropped, the dog shall be given the order to 'seek back' and must retrieve the article and return with speed. The dog may retrieve either by sight or scent."

All the above tests for the title U.D. are usually taken at an indoor or outdoor bench show. The tracking test, which is in the nature of a grand finale and would naturally attract a goodly crowd of onlookers, is unfortunately never held in connection with a show and so becomes a more or less exclusive and inconspicuous affair. It's just possible this is another reason why the U.D. award seems to have lost out in the pursuit race for popularity. Add the fact that only a few men and women have been licensed as qualified to officiate at this test and that opportunities to compete for the honor involved are necessarily limited in number, and you have two more possible explanations for lack of interest on the part of the average owner. But in case you happen to be intrigued with the prospect of owning a U.D. winner, here are the requirements:

Tracking must be performed with dog on leash, the distance to be covered to be not less than one-quarter mile long, the scent to be at least one-half hour old and that of a stranger who will leave the article to be found at the end of the track. The track should be plotted on the ground by the stewards on the day previous to the Tracking Test meeting when possible. The Tracklayers shall then follow the plotted tracks [on the following day], deposit the article to be found at the end of the track, and return over the track, collecting the marked pegs on the return journey, one peg not more than 30 yards from the commencement of the track to be left in, to indicate the direction of the track. The Tracklayers must not wear rubber-soled shoes. The length of the leash used in tracking shall be 30 or 40 feet in length and the dog shall work at this length with no help from his handler.

If this seems hopelessly technical and involved, stop and think a minute. To begin with, the tracking test is conducted at a spot where there is plenty of grass and soil to receive and retain scent, where a dog would nose about naturally and at a time when wind conditions are favorable. Then, too, the dog is worked on a leash or cord and so is always under control. Now consider what Jock *has already learned* in his retrieving lessons and you will realize the problems are by no means as difficult as they may appear. In the last three tests — scent discrimination, seeking back and tracking — you will find an ounce of observation worth a pound of rule reading. In fact, once you have seen any of the U.D. requirements competed for, you will probably be surprised at the simplicity rather than the intricacy of the routines. You will realize, as we have already said, that it is merely a case of adapting knowledge already acquired to certain specific conditions, no one of which is really difficult to meet.

As for standing for examination, all you need do is read the requirements and follow directions. Thousands of show dogs stand for examination every week of the year and do it perfectly; yet a goodly percentage of them have had no intensive training for it and many have never been handled by anyone making the slightest claim to ability as a trainer. The tracking test, which you conduct with your dog on leash, is not so simple. But any

dog with a half-decent nose will be able to fulfill
the conditions after a few weeks of training. If
he hasn't a half-decent nose he'll never be able to
qualify anyway, and there's nothing his owner
can do about it. The details of what training is
required you are now in a position to learn from
observation, talks with other handlers and fellow
exhibitors. As said in a previous chapter, the treatment of training for obedience tests in this book
must be, of necessity, comparatively sketchy. If
you use it to give Jock a good drilling in the
fundamentals he should at least win the C.D.
title. From that point on your contacts with men
and women in the obedience-test game will save
you trouble.

CHAPTER XXII

Consult Your Veterinarian

SINCE, for the purposes of this book, Jock is a composite dog, we have been obliged to assume all sorts of things about his mental, moral, emotional and physical make-up. Your individual Jock is sure to have some of these characteristics; but they will be comparatively few because so many contradict so many others that he would have to be a canine Dr. Jekyll and Mr. Hyde to have more than 50 per cent of them. But I have assumed one thing about Jock that is never true of any puppy and practically never of any grown dog. Up to this point I have taken it for granted that he is 100 per cent healthy and never needs a doctor.

Unfortunately I have no right to assume that to be the case, and, what is fully as important, should not assume that, when Jock is ailing, you are capable of diagnosing the trouble and deciding on the proper treatment. Long before you were born a famous American humorist wrote: "It's a darned sight better not to know so much than to know so many things that ain't so," and this horse-and-buggy-day philosophy is especially applicable to the amateur veterinarian.

Take worms, for instance. Why an all-wise Providence decreed that all puppies and most dogs should be pestered by worms is beyond me; but it certainly did. And just to make it more difficult for the owner Providence provided five distinct varieties, all with similar symptoms, yet each requiring entirely different treatment.

These varieties are tapeworms, round worms, hookworms, whipworms and heart worms. All but the last are fairly common. Practically every young puppy has round worms, which are white, vary in length from two or three inches to nearly a foot, and can usually be seen in the pup's feces or when he vomits them up. Whether you discover them or not Jock should be wormed on general principles when about two months old. Ask a reliable druggist for a first-class vermifuge for *puppy worms* and use it as per directions, repeating every eighteen to twenty-five days until you have given your pup four doses. From then on use it only when he shows definite symptoms or you find the worms in his stools. Vermifuges should always be given in the morning when the pup's or dog's stomach is practically empty.

The symptoms for all varieties of worms are so similar and, as already said, the proper treatments so different that, with the two exceptions of round worms and sometimes tapeworms, you should make no attempt to identify the species. Let a veterinarian examine the feces under his microscope, diagnose the case and prescribe. I can't make this too emphatic. Nearly all worm medicines are powerful and the wrong dose may do your young puppy serious harm. But this is an opportune time to repeat the statement made during the discussion of diet to the effect that a little garlic cut up fine and mixed with Jock's food every few days will be a wonderful help in keeping the worm situation under control.

Tapeworm segments, looking like small seeds, brown when dry and pink when fresh, are frequently to be found under or around the base of your pup's tail or you may discover them in the straw or shavings or on the sacking he uses for his bed. Since there are a number of varieties, consult your veterinarian before giving any treatment.

You should *suspect* the presence of *some species of worm* if Jock (1) is ravenously hungry; (2) is not hungry at all or has very little appetite; (3) looks fat and bloated, especially in the belly; (4) looks thin and scrawny; (5) has watery and what we call bleary eyes; (6) vomits frequently; (7) has chronic diarrhea; (8) passes blood in his movements; (9) has occasional fits; (10) has a harsh coat that lacks luster and has a tendency to stand erect rather than lie smooth and flat;

(11) passes worms, worm segments or worm eggs;
(12) coughs a great deal; (13) is listless;
(14) seems to have difficulty in breathing.

But once more, don't jump at conclusions.
Nearly all these symptoms may indicate something
quite different from worms and in many cases it
may be something much more serious. *Consult
your veterinarian.*

Among the more serious ailments many of the
above symptoms may suggest is distemper, almost
as common as worms and far more dangerous. It
is especially likely to attack puppies and is frequently fatal, since it readily runs into pneu-
monia or leaves aftereffects almost as bad. No dog,
whatever its age, who has not had the disease is
immune to it. A few years ago the dog that won
the award "Best in Show of All Breeds" at the
Westminster Kennel Club show in New York,
a fully grown English setter over a year old and
valued at thousands of dollars, came down with
it a month or two later. Despite the fact that he
was in superb physical condition, the attack was
so severe that, although he lived through it, he
has been shown very little since.

Distemper is especially serious because while
there is an anti-distemper serum that is supposed
to prevent it, no positive cure has ever been found.
To make matters worse, it is exceedingly con-
tagious. Its germs can be carried *for months* on

your clothing without losing their deadly efficiency and can be picked up by a dog in hundreds of ways you never suspect and so cannot prevent. And, to repeat what we have already said, the symptoms of the disease are so similar to those of other and less serious troubles they are easily passed over as comparatively unimportant. That's one of the prime reasons why the diagnoses of laymen when they have ailing puppies are so frequently wide of the mark. With the result that the disease gets off to a running start and by the time the owner suspects its presence it is too late. When your puppy or grown dog shows symptoms numbers 2, 5, 6, 7, 9, 12, 13, or 14 in the worm list, has fever, shivers or runs at the nose, take no chances — *consult your veterinarian.* In most cases he will not only prescribe for your dog but tell you how you can treat him at home.

I make no claims to medical knowledge, but I am firmly convinced that nine times out of ten distemper will not have serious or permanent results *if taken in time.* If ever the old proverb "An ounce of prevention is worth a pound of cure" was worth following, the treatment of canine distemper is an example. If you have the faintest idea Jock has been exposed to this disease, don't wait for its symptoms. Keep him in a warm, dry place that is free from drafts, don't allow him to exercise or get his feet wet, watch him as a broker watches his ticker tape in a jittery market and at the first slight indication of anything wrong, if it's only a little dumpiness, *send for your veterinarian.*

The reason I feel as I do about handling distemper by taking it in time is because I have seen how it works. In association with the late Mr. Richard B. Adams, I have raised a great many pups and kept scores of grown dogs. He taught me years ago that seeing trouble coming and meeting it halfway is a whole lot better than adopting the Bunker Hill system and "waiting until you see the whites of its eyes." Like all breeders, we had plenty of distemper to deal with. Indeed, we frequently picked a favorable time and deliberately exposed our dogs and pups to infection; but believe it or not, we never lost a single puppy or grown dog from the disease. Even granting this was partly due to phenomenal good luck, I still think the ounce of prevention we always kept on a figurative shelf in our kennels had a great deal to do with it.

If Jock has a fit you'll know it without asking any questions of anybody. There are a number of kinds, however. As usual send for the doctor. Before he arrives administer first aid yourself by throwing a blanket over the dog and, if possible, put him in a dark room where he can be alone and quiet down by himself, which he will probably do in a few minutes. If he's too big to handle get out of the way and let him go through with it. Incidentally don't become panicky and imagine it's a case of rabies. The violent stage of rabies does not come on suddenly, as do fits, and if you are even moderately observant you will see that something is radically wrong with your dog long before he becomes dangerous. If Jock has a fit when away from home throw your coat over him and if possible get him away from noise and crowds. If you are in your car, stop long enough to quiet him down, then take him directly to his kennel and call a veterinarian.

Rabies, exceedingly rare as a general thing, has two forms — violent and dumb. The primary symptoms of violent rabies are dumpiness and an attempt to get out of sight and be alone, or an equally unusual wish to be excessively petted and caressed. Or the dog may eat all sorts of things he has never touched before, show extreme nervousness and bark violently and continuously.

Dumb rabies is sometimes very similar in its early stages, but always entirely different as it progresses. But even from the first the dog with dumb rabies may show a peculiar drooping and semi-paralysis of the lower jaw, which will develop into complete paralysis later, and which keeps him from barking, makes it hard for him to swallow and also prevents him from biting as the disease nears its end and the dog dies.

There are inoculation treatments for the prevention of rabies. Their efficiency or lack of it is a subject for animated discussion whenever breeders meet, and even the doctors and laboratory experts are divided into two or three distinct schools on the question. One thing is sure: none of these treatments are for you to try on your own responsibility. So, for the sixth time in this chapter you get the warning: *send for your veterinarian* when your dog shows any or all the symptoms of either type of rabies.

Even if I knew the names of all the other ills that dogs are heir to and were competent to describe them and prescribe for them, I doubt if I would do so. It would be taking too much for granted. I've touched on worms, distemper and fits because they are very common among dogs, and mentioned rabies because, while it is very, very uncommon, fits are often mistaken for it and for that reason dogs that might easily be cured are unnecessarily put out of the way.

I'll simply add that milk of magnesia and glycerin suppositories will help overcome constipation and that mineral oil tends to keep the bowels regular; that dogs vomit easily and unless they do so frequently it probably means little unless accompanied by other symptoms; that occasional diarrhea is in the same class and can usually be cured by bismuth in a day or two. If it doesn't yield to treatment, watch out for worms or distemper. Also remember that puppies lose their baby teeth when five or six months old. This makes their gums tender and they need something fairly hard to chew on, like a bone. But they need bones anyway, so that suggestion should be superfluous.

Dogs that are kept constantly in warm rooms are likely to have skin troubles. So are all dogs that are not brushed vigorously every day or have little opportunity for good brisk exercise out of doors. Too frequent washing, as we have already said, will sometimes bring it on, too, since it takes the natural oil from the skin.

Eczema and mange are the two members of the skin-disease family that call most frequently. There are various varieties of eczema or skin infections commonly called by that name, but there are two kinds of the real thing — the dry and moist varieties. For the dry kind get from your druggist an ounce of Peru balsam, and a teaspoonful of creolin mixed with alcohol to fill an eight-ounce bottle. Apply it carefully to the skin without rubbing by using a soft rag. Put it on two or three times a day.

Moist eczema is moist and red instead of dry, and raw instead of scaly. Cut the hair of long-haired dogs where the eczema patches appear and apply a five per cent solution of tannic acid and salicylic acid in alcohol. Give the dog a good bath after you have finished with the treatments, then rub into the coat a 50–50 mixture of cocoanut oil and olive oil to restore the oiliness necessary to a healthy skin.

Mange, both sarcoptic and follicular, is too tough a problem for you to handle and since the symptoms are almost the same as those of dry eczema, it should be by this time unnecessary to suggest tactfully that, if you don't get results in treating either dry or moist eczema within a couple of weeks, it would be a good idea to call or write *your veterinarian.*

Now that we have given the doctor plenty to do, we'll finish with something you yourself can do and that you will always or nearly always be doing — trying to free Jock of fleas.

No matter how aristocratic Jock's lineage or how classy the kennel or individual breeder from whom you got him, he had at least a few fleas or their eggs concealed on his person when he came to you. No matter how continuously you brush and groom him and how diligently you search for the little jokers during all the years you own him, he will still be harboring a few when you bid him a last good-bye. But they can be kept under almost complete control with very little trouble.

A good stiff brushing every day annoys even the

most blasé flea no end and he will be inclined to leave Jock for another dog whose master or mistress is less industrious. If you give the dog a bath (two teaspoonfuls of creolin to a gallon of water) now and then, followed by a thorough going over with a fine-tooth comb, you will be able to keep the situation well in hand. This goes for lice, too, which are not so universally and everlastingly present and unaccounted for as fleas, but can be very irritating.

That's all for ailments and insect pests with the exception of two pathological conditions which you may not recognize as ailments but which are in reality nervous disorders so serious they require separate chapters. These are man-shyness and timidity in general, and the very unusual diseases we call viciousness and cowardice.

CHAPTER XXIII

Man-Shyness and Timidity in General

TIMID and man-shy dogs present a serious and exasperating problem. Serious because timidity is usually inborn and for that reason exceedingly hard to overcome; exasperating because such dogs run counter to our conception of what all normal dogs should be.

Fortunately intelligent fanciers know shyness is hereditary and conscientiously breed it out. But there are occasional dealers who are neither intelligent nor conscientious and the average amateur breeder is blissfully ignorant of the wrong he does when he sells a timid pup. With the result that many an owner discovers too late that his or her affection is not only unappreciated but possibly actually resented. This is a real tragedy and such disappointed owners deserve both sympathy and assistance.

If your pup is young enough, you have a sporting chance for his cure. Grown dogs with the fear complex are, in my experience, almost hopeless. I'll admit I came near curing a fully grown female named Meg some years ago, but it was attempted as an experiment and the process took an immense amount of time and patience. Since this was a typical case a brief résumé of what happened will be instructive.

Meg grew up in a big kennel yard with nine or ten other pups, and as long as she was inside the inclosure never showed the slightest sign of shyness. Whenever anyone, friend or stranger, stood just outside the yard fence, she would rush up with the other pups to be petted, wag her tail hysterically and, in a word, act as any normal dog would do. She felt absolutely safe in her familiar surroundings; and the fact that nine out of ten timid dogs feel exactly the same way under similar circumstances makes it easy for unscrupulous breeders to hoodwink buyers and get rid of such undesirables at good prices.

In Meg's case she was almost never out of that yard until she was more than a year old, when I decided to take her down to my house for training. From the moment she arrived she was afraid of the house itself and everything and everybody in it. The only room she felt halfway comfortable in was my den; and the only person she could endure the sight of was myself — not that she liked me more, but that she liked the other members of the family less.

For nearly a week she absolutely refused to be coaxed out of the den. Since she was not housebroken I had to drag her outdoors at the end of a leash. She lay in that room hour after hour, trembling almost constantly and only occasionally taking her eyes off me as I worked at my desk. Apparently she was waiting for some catastrophe she felt was coming — and it always came. If it wasn't a tin baking dish dropped on the kitchen floor near by, it was the closing of a door or someone stepping into the room, or even looking in. The clicking keys of my typewriter terrified her.

Since the handling of this typewriter situation was signally successful and the principle involved applies to anything that frightens a timid dog, I'll explain it.

If I had stopped typing, crossed to Meg, patted her and told her everything was all right, it would in all probability have made a bad matter worse. She would have felt I realized the typewriter was dangerous and was apologizing for using it. There was only one logical thing to do — utterly ignore both Meg and her terror and *keep on pounding those keys.*

That's what I did and here's what happened. Within two days Meg would relax the minute I began working, stretch herself out on her rug and go to sleep. She had found out for herself that the supposed infernal machine was not only harmless as her feed pan but actually soothing to her nerves. While she would still waken and start nervously at other sounds, they seemed to frighten her less when the keys were clicking.

Conditions in this particular case were exceptionally unfavorable because the dog was inactive physically and had nothing on her mind but her fears. The chances are you will accustom your pup to strange sounds by deliberately making them, just as I did; but you will probably improve on my tactics by choosing a time when he is busy with something in which he is intensely interested. In that case he may not notice that noise at all, or, if he does, he may be much less afraid of it.

Old-time trainers of bird dogs used a modification of this system in curing gun-shyness, a highly specialized and very persistent form of timidity. They used to fire a pistol over the pup when he was eating his dinner. If the youngster was frightened and retreated into its barrel or box, they took the food away, waited until the next feeding time and repeated the program. To put it baldly, they tried to starve the pup out of his fright. The modern trainer has discarded this cruel practice for another, identical in principle but perfectly humane. He sees to it timid pups hear the report of a firearm for the first time when they are gaily chasing flushed game or are hot on the trail of feathers or fur. He is careful, too, to begin with a cap pistol or small rifle rather than a shotgun, working up to the louder report by easy stages.

You can profit by his example. Pick a time when your pup is busy with his dinner, playing with your old glove or chasing a bird or butterfly, and make your first noises slight ones like the snap of a lighting match.

Since timidity is often little more than extreme nervousness, a change of diet, more exercise and a reasonable amount of time may bring a cure. But remember Meg. Don't even suggest to your pup you have the least idea he *is* timid. Slowly but surely he may begin to share your own indifference to strange sights and sounds.

This advice relates more especially to ordinary shyness. Man-shyness is an aggravated form much more difficult to handle. No system can be guaranteed, but the one most likely to bring results is to take advantage of a trait common to all dogs, extreme jealousy. Your man-shy pup not only doesn't crave your company or caresses; he does everything in his power to escape them. But he's in a state of mind when he sees you making a fuss over another dog. This characteristic may be your anchor to windward. Again Meg is interesting as an example.

When I brought her to the house I had there an almost perfect house dog named Nip. He had never been spoiled by too much petting, but by the time Meg had been in the family a few days he must have thought I was suffering from a severe attack of senile dementia. I used to sit in the kitchen, where Meg could see me through an open door, pat the puzzled Nip on the head for fifteen minutes at a stretch and tell him he was a good dog until I felt like a congenital idiot. But it worked. Miss Timidity would watch us, green-eyed, run to the kitchen door, put her paw over the threshold, draw it back again, whine with mingled jealousy and fright, go back to her rug in my den and begin watching us again. Finally she could no longer stand the strain; she simply had to get in on that petting party. One day out into the kitchen she came.

The first few times she didn't stay three seconds, but she got her pat on the head and liked it because it meant one less pat for Nip. Gradually she began to get the habit and the rest was easy insofar as I personally was concerned. Her fear of the rest of the family still persisted, but when, one by one, they played my role in the ridiculous little farce, Meg began to become somewhere near normal.

When she was accidentally killed three months later she was well on her way to a complete cure. She was an exceptional specimen physically and if she had lived might have done considerable winning at the bench shows; but if she had become an international champion I would never have allowed her a litter of pups. Her hereditary taint was too strong.

Meg's case was extreme. If you will follow the fundamentals illustrated in her attempted reformation — ignore your pup's fears and make full use of his jealousy — you will in all probability get quicker results than I did. If you have no second dog for bait, you may be able to borrow one or take your pup to the house of a friend who has a dog he or she will contribute to the cause. The latter is an excellent plan because, when away from home, the pup will probably turn to you for protection against strangers, and will be much more jealous of your attentions to an unknown dog in an unfamiliar place than of the same sort of attentions given in his own home to a dog he knows. He may figure you have deserted him entirely for this new applicant for your affections. Little as he trusts you, he will consider this a calamity.

Whether at home or abroad, never allow strangers to approach a man-shy puppy quickly or unexpectedly. This may sound difficult, but the use of ordinary judgment will take care of the situation without embarrassment to anyone concerned. It's no disgrace to own a timid puppy and there's no reason why you should not tell visitors about his failing and that you are trying to overcome it. On the street your acquaintances will understand equally well and act accordingly when warned to help you out by not being too effusive. It's best that callers and people you meet on the street leave the pup entirely unnoticed. Timid dogs sometimes resent being ignored just as shy people do. If allowed a little time to think things over your pup may make a cautious bid for a little attention and appreciate it when he gets it.

With grown dogs this course is of especial importance for a different reason. "Barking dogs never bite" is in the main true, and so is its opposite. Shy dogs, which very rarely bark, do bite at times. This is not because they are vicious. They snap, if at all, only when they are taken by surprise, consider themselves in danger and cornered, and act in self-defense. But a dog bite is a dog bite and explanations are usually wasted breath. Even if the owner is fortunate enough to escape a doctor's bill or lawsuit, his position is far from enviable.

Conversely, when you approach a strange dog that you suspect is shy, as you may frequently find it necessary to do, go toward him slowly and quietly. When you are near enough stop, and, if necessary, crouch and hold out your hand, palm up, as a sign of good will.

One final tip. When your once-timid pup begins to like and trust you don't make the mistake of treating him too gently. Use your very best judgment and when you feel the time is ripe begin romping and playing with him, confining your petting to a pat on the head now and then. Begin by throwing a ball, for instance, and let the game grow gradually rougher as time goes on. In treating convalescent cases you'll find a little good-natured cuffing has coddling and baby talk stopped.

CHAPTER XXIV

Vicious and Cowardly Dogs

I WISH I could omit this chapter, but I cannot conscientiously do so. Timid dogs are by no means uncommon; cowardly and vicious dogs are extremely rare. But they exist; and since they are a menace to mankind and may bring their owners lasting regret and heavy financial loss, it is only fair to sound a warning such owners will do well to heed.

We have already said that as a rule the dog is the one so-called dumb animal whose intelligence does not make him dangerous. Cowardly and naturally vicious dogs are the rare exceptions that prove that rule. The fact that dogs are among the cleverest of animals and that, when abnormal and criminally inclined, they are abnormally cunning and crafty makes them a serious menace to mankind. Such dogs may be models of all the canine virtues when their masters or mistresses are at hand and dangerous characters when by themselves and on their own.

After all, the prehistoric dog was carnivorous, killing and eating its prey. The domestic dog is

still carnivorous and in some cases potentially sav-
age, as witness the so-called "wild dogs," direct
descendants of household pets, but which have
gone native and become almost as bloodthirsty
and, very significantly, as cowardly, as wolves. For
they are bold and dangerous only when running
in packs. Such packs have been known to attack
not only livestock and children, but adults as
well.

There is a vitally important lesson in this. A
good dog, like a good man or woman, is an object
of affection and admiration, a challenge and an in-
spiration. A congenitally bad dog is just the opposite. We put our human criminals under lock
and key and our insane where they can do no
harm to themselves or others. Yet you and I have
seen dogs as vicious as any human gangster or as
mentally unsound as the village half-wit, whose
doting owners not only allowed them to run
at large, but actually condoned their crimes or
refused to admit they were crimes at all.
Such owners are worse than their dogs. Through
their ignorance or blind refusal to face the
facts the vast majority of dogs — those that are
gentle, kindly and altogether admirable — suffer
for the sins of the few that are treacherous and
unsafe.

If your pet is perfectly kind and dependable
insofar as you and yours are concerned but not to

be trusted with strangers, even if they are guests in your home, he is abnormal and dangerous. Make sure he is given no opportunity to harm man or beast. To permit him to roam the streets or countryside or even to allow him the liberty of your own premises is riding for a fall in the form of heavy damages or a heavier heart when you find yourself responsible for the serious and it may be permanent injury of someone who trusted an untrustworthy and so worse than worthless dog.

Of course the above does not apply to the comparatively few dogs kept for the express purpose of protecting one's person or property, acting as night watchmen at mills or as bodyguards for men who customarily deal with dangerous characters. Such dogs are usually *deliberately taught to be vicious,* and nine times out of ten show remarkable discrimination in the discharge of their duty. They seem to know criminals from honest men by instinct and seldom attack the latter.

Even with dogs of this type there should be no misunderstanding as to their character. If you have such a dog to accompany and assist you in your work, let it be publicly known that he will allow no familiarities; if he is the guardian of your property give trespassers fair warning by means of a conspicuously placed sign. These simple and reasonable precautions put your dog in the class to which he belongs and place no stigma on dogs in general or on you.

In all fairness to man's best friend it should be said that viciousness, while many times inborn, is much less frequently so than timidity or man-shyness. It is too often the result of ill-treatment of a pup by its master or by others. Continued and senseless teasing, already mentioned, will some-times cause it. So will habitual beatings. Cruel owners make cruel dogs. Many a pup, naturally good-natured and trustworthy, has grown up to be a public enemy through no fault of his own. Be kind to your young puppy and the chances are overwhelmingly in favor of his growing up to be a kindly dog.

Man-shy, timid and vicious dogs are, as we have seen, extremely undesirable. The first two are annoying, disappointing and occasionally even dangerous in a mild way. The third is annoying, disappointing and definitely dangerous. Worse than all three put together is the cowardly dog. He is not only annoying, disappointing and dan-gerous — he is despicable.

Shy dogs deserve a certain amount of sympathy; vicious dogs may inspire a degree of respect; but cowardly dogs, like cowardly men, are low-down sneaks and should not be tolerated under any cir-cumstances whatever. Man-shyness and timidity may sometimes be cured; viciousness may be controlled or even put to a useful purpose. Cowardice is, in my opinion, incurable. Once a coward always a coward; and a coward can have no redeeming feature or features important enough to make up for that one unforgivable fault.

What are the distinguishing characteristics of a cowardly dog? A good way to answer that question is to describe his opposite, a courageous one, a typical terrier for example. We have already said he will tackle anything. He never learns caution and physical pain only makes him fight the harder. He is always perfectly willing to go out of his class in both size and weight for the sake of a good scrap and likes to pick an opponent bigger and stronger than he is. When it comes to killing rats, for instance, it's obvious he considers it just a job, not a fight. He'd rather tackle a good big woodchuck any time because the 'chuck is a punishing fighter when cornered and has a sporting chance. I have seen a wirehair kill a woodchuck practically his own size, when the 'chuck's teeth had so wicked a hold on the terrier's lower jaw that they completely pierced it and locked in a vise-like grip. The dog's pain must have been excruciating but the nervy little gamester never winced, and actually used his opponent's hold to shake him into semi-insensibility so that he could give him the *coup de grâce*.

Whenever possible terriers give fair warning

and attack from the front. It may have been necessary to use stealth in stalking that woodchuck,
for instance. If he had seen the terrier in time he
would have made for his hole hell-bent for protection and the dog would have been robbed of
the fun of a fight. But the wirehair's thrill came
when his quarry was cornered and turned at bay,
not, as in the case of a hound, when he was chasing it.

That's why terriers are such inveterate barkers.
They bark to attract the attention of other animals they cannot reach, but which they hope will
accept the challenge, come to them and have it
out. They bark almost as violently at people,
too, as almost anyone who has ever visited the
owner of one can testify. But that they do it
good-naturedly as a greeting or simply to force
you to notice them is evident from the furry
blur of their stubby tails as they wag a welcome.

If a terrier happens to have a vicious streak,
which is very rarely the case, he gives fair warning, attacks from the front and flies at you like
a little fury, just as he does at his four-legged
foes. Yet he scorns so much as to threaten a child.
He seems to realize its helplessness and does not
consider it a foeman worthy of his teeth.

Now let's compare the terrier's code of honor
with the conduct of a cowardly dog. When we do,

we find every article of the coward's creed diametrically opposite the terrier's.

The canine coward is very seldom a little fellow. Like small men, small dogs are inclined to be pugnacious. It's usually narrow shoulders, not big broad ones, that carry the chips; and the reverse is equally true. Cowardly dogs are usually good-sized specimens abundantly able to take care of themselves in a set-to with dogs of their weight and inches, but they haven't the nerve to try it. So they pick on little dogs and sidestep arguments with their physical equals.

To continue the comparison, cowards never give fair warning of an intended attack, whether on man or beast. They lie in wait behind a protecting bush or around a convenient corner until their unsuspecting victims have passed and they can come on them stealthily from the rear. Even then they have no stomach for a fair stand-up, give-and-take fight, but are satisfied with a quick snap at a leg followed by a hasty retreat if the bitten party turns and faces them.

As a general thing cowards bark but little, since, as we have said, barking is for two purposes: to give fair warning, which cowards never do, or to attract attention, which cowards seldom crave. The rare occasions when they do voice a challenge to other dogs or an apparent ultimatum to humans to keep their distance are usually under conditions that make the coward consider it impossible for the dog to accept the challenge or the human to reach him and call his bluff. If the barker discovers he was mistaken in either of these assumptions he stops barking, drops his tail and slinks out of the danger zone as quickly and unobtrusively as he can.

Finally, cowardly dogs sometimes stoop so low as to attack children. For this reason alone, if for no other, they merit no mercy and should receive none. If you are unfortunate enough to own a dog of this kind, I have only this to say, and I can't say it too emphatically. The slightest injury inflicted on an innocent child by your cowardly dog or mine outweighs all other considerations. Even if he is a pampered household pet, he should be turned over to a veterinarian, given a dose of chloroform and painlessly but permanently put out of circulation.

What is the difference between a cowardly dog and a timid one? You have already figured it for yourself. Timid dogs may occasionally bite, but only when they consider it necessary for self-defense. They *never* attack a human being or another dog from behind. They do not pick on smaller dogs for the reason that they are just as afraid of small dogs as they are of big ones. They never bark a challenge to a fight as a bluff. They are on the level in that respect and frankly admit they are timid. And they almost never snap at children because they are not afraid of them as they are of grown people. All in all, they are more to be pitied than censured.

You may have noticed I have not mentioned Jock so much as once in the last two chapters. That is by design, not accident. Since you chose him as a pup with his disposition in mind and have treated him with kindness and common sense ever since, *he is neither man-shy, timid, vicious nor cowardly*. But you may have a friend or acquaintance unfortunate enough to own a dog that is one of the four. It is with the hope that you may be of assistance to this greatly-to-be-pitied man or woman that this and the preceding chapter are included in this book.

CHAPTER XXV

"The Best of Friends Must Part"

I AM sincerely sorry that the time has come to say "Good-bye and good luck!" During the writing of this book I have come to feel I know you and Jock personally and intimately. I have even taken the liberty of assuming you are my friend, as I am yours, and that Jock is a true and loyal friend of us both. In fact, it seems that, without my realizing it, you and Jock have become to me an ideal master and dog. Which means you are much cleverer, more observing, tactful, patient and efficient than I have ever been or can hope to be. So perhaps you will be interested to know that thinking of you brings to my mind an actual flesh-and-blood friend whom I knew for many years and whom I like to imagine you resemble in your attitude toward Jock and dogs in general. I'm not going to mention his name for two reasons: he was so modest and retiring that, if he were still living, he would never forgive me; and if I did, you would be none the wiser, for his reputation was, by his own preference, purely local. I'm simply going to tell you two little anecdotes that illustrate, I think, how thoroughly a naturally sympathetic, intelligent and *observant* man or woman with a real love for dogs can understand them and their nature. For the sake of convenience I'll call this friend George Spelvin. If you happen to know the traditions of the American theater you will know why I choose that name and it may hand you an amused smile.

I met him in the summer of 1916. I had a setter pup I wanted trained for gunning, and as I lived in the city at that time and was very busy had no chance to handle the job myself. Someone told me Spelvin was the best man in ten counties to do it for me, so I drove up to his modest little farmhouse to break the ice. Break the ice, I discovered, was right. George was not exactly what we call "chatty" with strangers. But when I left for home he had somehow given me the impression that, if he found my hopeful worth bothering about, he might possibly get around to doing a little something with him. I could bring the pup up to the farm and in the meantime he'd be thinking it over.

The next day I put little Rowdy in the car and we stopped off at Spelvin's again. When I left it was all settled. Not that George said so in so many words, but I understood New Englanders well enough to know the deal was on. And I knew something else: either the man was an arrant fraud, which I couldn't believe, or I had met the most amazing dog psychiatrist I had ever seen.

The way of it was this. While Spelvin and I were talking, Rowdy was rambling about the place, nosing here and there, lapping up a little leftover milk from a battered feed dish, chasing an occasional chicken and, in a word, acting exactly as all adolescent bird dogs have always acted. I had expected the man to give the little tyke a careful going-over; but with the exception of an occasional glance out of the tail of his eye, he never seemed to know the pup was on the premises. Yet, as I was leaving, he came out with a speech so surprising I can still repeat it almost word for word.

"Well, I'll tell you, Mister," he said slowly in his typical Yankee way, "this pup of yours has got a better'n average nose and he's going to be good and staunch on his birds. He'll handle nice and easy, too; but at the same time there's nothing timid about him and he'll be a good free mover in the brush and bold and independent-like when he's hunting. But of course you know all about that already."

He waited for me to agree or disagree, but I was too taken aback to answer, so he went on musingly, as if talking to himself.

"And another thing: He's going to cut up his ground in good shape, and he'll be no trailer. He'll carry his head high, the way he should, and get the scent of his game out of the air instead of off the ground. He's going to be a mighty practical grouse dog on that account, because he'll point as soon as he gets body scent and you can walk up to him and steady him down by talking to him. Not only that; you can give him a little taste of the switch, when he deserves it, without breaking his spirit and making him sour. Taking him all around and barring accidents, I wouldn't wonder if you'd get a good useful dog out of him."

Now unless you happen to be something of a gunner, Spelvin's talk may seem a bit technical; but it's not too technical for you to realize he was giving me a complete and detailed psychoanalysis of what my six-months-old pup would be when a mature and thoroughly trained dog. Also that he was doing this without even speaking to the pup or throwing more than a casual glance in his direction now and then.

Did his predictions come true? Of course they did, or I shouldn't be writing about them. How could Spelvin isolate and identify all those characteristics? Simply by making the most of a native knack for *seeing things* — not merely looking at them — and by drawing conclusions from what he saw. Add to this the fact that his instinctive insight into dog psychology made his conclusions sound, and you have the answer.

He knew Rowdy had a good nose on account of the distance from which he caught the scent of that milk in the feed pan; and the way he worked up to and located it showed he would hunt with a good high head later on. He knew the pup was naturally staunch because he saw him hold a point on one of those broilers for a moment or two before his enthusiasm got the better of him and he dashed in to chase the chick. When I called sharply to stop him from catching the bird, his reactions were the tip-off that he would be easy to handle without being timid; in other words, they showed he had the temperament to stand a little punishment when and if it should ever be necessary. Rowdy's work on the chicken scent showed, too, how he would cover his ground when searching for game and gave added evidence of the fact that he was neither a trailer nor a potterer.

This little story illustrates Spelvin's gift for getting inside a dog's head, watching the wheels go round and figuring what makes them whirl and why. Now for an example of observation, pure and simple, with no deductions involved. It may not be especially surprising, but, to you as a dog owner, it should be interesting.

One afternoon I happened to be at the Spelvin farm when a stranger stopped to inquire the way to the Swingalong Kennels, eight or nine miles to the north. In his car was a pointer female he was planning to breed to one of the Swingalong dogs. She was as sweet a little piece of dog flesh as you would wish to see, and while George was giving her owner the route to the kennels, I gave her a thorough inspection with what I then considered my expert eye. This was twenty years ago.

When Spelvin had the stranger straightened out as to his road, he left us both flat and went to the barn to begin his milking. I took the opportunity to ask the man about the hunting qualities of his dog, and when he told me she was a knockout on birds, I was sold hook, line and sinker and said I might buy one of her prospective pups, if the price was right.

A few minutes after the man had driven away, Spelvin came from the barn and I gave him an earful about the wonderful qualities of that pointer and told him my idea about buying one of her pups.

George just looked at me with that good-natured smile of his and I was silly enough to resent it.

"What's the matter?" I asked. "Don't you agree with me?"

"Sure! Sure I do," he said tactfully. "Only, if I were you, I wouldn't get all steamed up over buying one of those pups of hers."

"No? Why not?"

"Well, of course I don't know much about her

one way or another, but I don't figure she'll *have* any pups, not more than one or two anyway. To my way of thinking she's just a trifle too old."

"Old? How old do you think she is?"

"I wouldn't want to say exactly — somewhere between eleven and twelve, isn't she? You noticed her teeth, didn't you?"

No, I hadn't noticed her teeth and I couldn't imagine how *he* had. Come to find out, she had opened her mouth to yawn and he "just happened to be looking." That was George any time, any place. He always "just happened to be looking."

But he wasn't through with that pointer. Ten minutes later he came back to her again.

"Speaking of that dog," he said, "she may be a sure-enough knockout in the brush but she hasn't been hunted much — not this season anyhow."

As I had told George she was in great hunting condition — hard as nails — this was something of a slam at my judgment, but I knew he didn't mean it that way.

"You're probably right," I said, "but how do you figure it?"

"Same as you would, I guess. Maybe you might have forgotten to look at her toenails."

Sold again! Simple Simon should have seen that her nails were long and sharp and realized that even a fair amount of work during the season would have made them short and stubby. I had overlooked it — but not Spelvin, even though he had seemed so uninterested he had annoyed me a little. He never overlooked anything — except the failings of his friends.

As you will infer from these two incidents Spelvin was a bird-dog specialist, but his ability to size up a dog of any breed was just as uncanny. I took his opinion of a Pomeranian as quickly and with as little question as I took his estimate of a pointer. Because he *knew dogs* up, down, across and through the middle. You may be as good as or better than he, but, in any case, you will understand why he could get more out of a dog in less time and with less apparent effort than anyone I have ever seen.

But his success in handling dogs was based on something even more important. During all the years I knew him I saw him disappointed, disgusted and even thoroughly angry inside at times, but I never saw him discouraged and I never saw him lose his poise or self-control. Which brings me to the good old moth-eaten motto that should hang on every owner's wall and be woven into his consciousness like the "Welcome" on his doormat:

NEVER LOSE YOUR TEMPER.

Jock will never lose his, and he's only a dog.

PUREBRED DOGS IN THE UNITED STATES

Listed in Six Groups, as Officially Classified by the American Kennel Club

GROUP I

Sporting Dogs

Griffons (Wire-haired Pointing)
Pointers
Pointers (German Short-haired)
Retrievers (Chesapeake Bay)
Retrievers (Curly-coated)
Retrievers (Flat-coated)
Retrievers (Golden)
Retrievers (Labrador)
Setters (English)
Setters (Gordon)
Setters (Irish)
Spaniels (American Water)
Spaniels (Brittany)
Spaniels (Clumber)
Spaniels (Cocker, American Type)
Spaniels (Cocker, English Type)
Spaniels (English Springer)
Spaniels (Field)
Spaniels (Irish Water)
Spaniels (Sussex)
Spaniels (Welsh Springer)

GROUP II

Sporting Dogs — Hounds

Afghan Hounds
Basset Hounds
Beagles
Bloodhounds
Borzoi (Russian Wolfhounds)
Dachshunde
Deerhounds (Scottish)
Foxhounds (American)
Foxhounds (English)
Greyhounds
Harriers
Norwegian Elkhounds
Otterhounds
Salukis
Whippets
Wolfhounds (Irish)

GROUP III

WORKING DOGS

Alaskan Malemutes
Bernese Mountain Dogs
Bouviers des Flandres
Boxers
Briards
Bull-Mastiffs
Collies (Rough)
Collies (Smooth)
Doberman Pinschers
Eskimo Dogs
German Shepherd Dogs
Great Danes
Great Pyrenees
Komondorock

Kuvasz
Mastiffs
Newfoundlands
Pulis
Rottweilers
Samoyedes (Spitz)
Schnauzers (Giant)
Sheep Dogs (Belgian)
Sheep Dogs (Old English)
Sheep Dogs (Shetland)
Siberian Huskies
Saint Bernards
Welsh Corgis (Cardigan)
Welsh Corgis (Pembroke)

GROUP IV

TERRIERS

Airedale Terriers
Bediington Terriers
Border Terriers
Bullterriers (White and
    Colored)
Cairn Terriers
Dandie Dinmont Terriers
Fox Terriers (Smooth and
    Wire)
Irish Terriers
Kerry Blue Terriers
Lakeland Terriers

Lhasa Terriers
Manchester Terriers
Norwich Terriers
Schnauzers (Miniature and
    Standard)
Scottish Terriers
Sealyham Terriers
Skye Terriers
Staffordshire Terriers
Welsh Terriers
West Highland White
    Terriers

GROUP V

Toy Dogs

Affenpinschers
Chihuahuas
Griffons (Brussels)
Italian Greyhounds
Maltese
Mexican Hairless
Papillons
Pekinese

Pinschers (Miniature)
Pomeranians
Pugs
Spaniels (English Toy)
Spaniels (Japanese)
Terriers (Toy Manchester)
Terriers (Yorkshire)
Toy Poodles

GROUP VI

Non-Sporting Dogs

Boston Terriers
Bulldogs
Chow Chows
Dalmatians

French Bulldogs
Keeshonden
Poodles (Standard)
Schipperkes

INDEX